MODELS AND ECONOMIC THEORY

IVY PAPPS, Ph.D.
Department of Economics,
University of Durham,
Durham, England

WILLIE HENDERSON, M.A.
Institute of Education
University of Keele,
Keele, England

1977
W. B. SAUNDERS COMPANY
Philadelphia, London, Toronto

W. B. Saunders Company: West Washington Square
Philadelphia, PA 19105

1 St. Anne's Road
Eastbourne, East Sussex BN21 3UN, England

1 Goldthorne Avenue
Toronto, Ontario M8Z 5T9, Canada

Library of Congress Cataloging in Publication Data

Papps, Ivy,

Models and economic theory.

Bibliography: p.

1. Economics — Mathematical models.   I. Henderson,
   Willie, joint author.   II. Title.

HB141.P36   330'.01'51   76–20103
ISBN 0–7216–7063–6

Cover illustration titled *Planned City* is enamel on steel by Virgil Cantini

Models and Economic Theory   ISBN 0-7216-7063-6

Last digit is the print number: 9   8   7   6   5   4   3   2   1

PREFACE

This book is aimed primarily, but not exclusively, at students taking their first course in economics. We feel that it could also yield benefits to students starting their studies in other social sciences—and perhaps even to those in the physical sciences.

Although a treatment as extensive as that presented here is novel, teachers of introductory economics have come to accept that it is desirable to introduce students to some rudimentary concepts of scientific methodology at the beginning of their course. Hence, the great increase in "principles" texts that devote the first chapter or two to this subject. Many teachers believe that such a cursory treatment is sufficient. We have been moved to write this book, however, by the conviction, based on our teaching experience, that the usual short treatment in the conventional textbooks not only is insufficient but also often confuses rather than clarifies the important points *as seen by the student.*

This last point is crucial. Much of the experience used in the writing of this book was gained during a research project into the problems of teaching and learning basic economics that was undertaken at the University of Sussex in England. One of the results of this project was the realization that students often enter the study of economics with expectations of the subject that differ from those of their teachers. Moreover, there is little during the first few months of their course that can help them to evaluate their expectations or to revise them intelligently.

The results of this confusion are familiar to many teachers of economics. Students become alienated from the study of economic theory because they feel that the assumptions of economics are unrealistic (and, as a result, that the theory cannot be used for the formation of the economic and social policy in which many of them are interested); because they feel that the distinction between positive and normative questions is unreal and perhaps even "immoral"; because they find the insistence on the *prediction* of human behavior both grandiose and vaguely menacing. The list could be extended by many more examples. The effect on the teacher of such alienation is clear: It makes the teaching of economics much more difficult. For the student, it makes it more difficult to learn. It is also clear that many of these difficulties are a result of a failure to communicate clearly to the student an understanding of what economists are actually doing when they build their elegant models. The conventional short treatment in the "principles" textbooks has, in many cases, been worse than useless because it hides the difficulties and ambiguities and presents the case for the use of scientific methodology with no room for argument. In recognition of this point, it should be noted that John Lindauer's book, to which this is a companion volume, omits any discussion of methodology.

This book attempts to go further than the conventional discussion. It starts at a lower conceptual level than is usual, and it discusses both the purposes and the methods of simplification. This subject is not usually discussed because the teacher considers it all too obvious. Yet we have discovered that students are often most disturbed by those aspects of model-building directly related to simplification. It is not at all obvious to students that it is desirable to simplify. "Ceteris paribus" is simply anathema to many students. We discuss simplification in some detail in an attempt to help them to understand both its benefits *and its costs*. In this way we hope to provide students with the apparatus with which to judge intelligently the kinds of simplifications involved in economic analysis.

Because of the nature of the subject, the discussion in this book will frequently appear circular and repetitious. This is deliberate. The subject *is* circular and can really only be understood as a whole. It is not easily reduced to the linear treatment imposed by the written word. So accepting the limitations of our medium, we have chosen to use extensively a system of cross-references — both forward and backward.

A last word to the student: You may feel that this book is propaganda to persuade you to accept the use of models. Of course, this is true. We would not have chosen to write this book if we had not hoped to persuade you of this. It is not our primary purpose, however. Our primary purpose is to provide you with some tools with which you can critically and intelligently evaluate particular models or the practice of model-building. If you ultimately decide to reject models, we hope that you will have learned some convincing arguments with which to do so.

We must thank our colleagues at the University of Sussex, with whom we had many invaluable discussions at all stages of the project — many of them long before the book was conceived. In particular, we thank Paul Chalmers-Dixon, John Field, Norman MacKenzie, John McKay, Peter Morris, and Terry Ryan for long discussions in which we gained many ideas, and in which we were induced to consider our own ideas more carefully. John Albery, Kitty Zangara Henderson, and Percy Selwyn also provided a great deal of help throughout the project through long and numerous conversations full of criticisms and ideas. Many of these people will disagree with some parts of this book, but it could not have been written without them. Students too numerous to mention here have helped us with critical discussions of various aspects. We must also thank John Aidem, James Crawford, John and Jacqueline Lindauer, and Margaret Naumes for their painstaking comments on earlier drafts of the manuscript. Any mistakes that may remain after all this help are, of course, our own.

CONTENTS

8

9

LOOKING AT MODELS

1

A fashion model; an artist's model; a model airplane; Henry Ford's model T; a model of an Indian village; a model child. All are familiar to us. Yet what possible connection could they have with economic theory? Indeed, apart from the obvious fact that they all contain the word "model," what connections are there between them?

These connections are essentially the subject of this book. While models are useful in everyday life and are more common than one might initially think, they are also the very basis of all scientific inquiry. Before looking at their use in science, however, it is helpful to have a more precise idea of what models are and what they do. Without them one would find it difficult to engage in even the simplest activity.

WHAT IS A MODEL?

In our day-to-day lives we are constantly using models. Some we do recognize explicitly as such.

A fashion model wears clothes to give other people some idea of how the clothes would look on them. Although the fashion model cannot show exactly how the clothes will look on another person who does not have the same physique, there is usually enough information to deduce this. This kind of model does more than provide information about clothes; he or she is also an ideal—a person to admire and perhaps to envy.

An artist's model is also a real person: an original that is copied by the artist. The copy is seldom a complete reproduction—the artist omits some details because his purpose is not simply reproduction but is rather the creation of a new work of art.

A model airplane is usually a copy of an existing aircraft. Again it omits details, usually because it is smaller than the original. Many models are of this type: model cars, model soldiers, model ships, and so on. Sometimes such models are built before the originals to help designers test various facets of the design.

The model T was a *type* of automobile rather than a miniature reproduction of one. This usage of the word has continued to apply to varieties of automobiles, televisions, radios, and other kinds of consumer durables.

Like the model airplane, the model of the Indian village is a scale copy that omits some details because of its size. Unlike the model airplane, this model is not a copy of a *particular* Indian village. It picks out and illustrates the important features of most Indian villages. It is, therefore, not a representation of a particular village but a classification system showing the features usually found in Indian villages.

A model child differs the most from the other types of models. From the parent's point of view, a model child is the best possible child. Similarly, a model student is the best possible student from the teacher's point of view. The essential feature of this use of the word is that certain characteristics are picked out as being the most desirable in a certain situation.

These six familiar uses of the word model do differ, but certain common features are beginning to emerge.

Definitions

A model that recommends certain characteristics is called a *normative* model. Other models that just simplify the original are called *positive* models.

First, all models tell us something about another object. The fashion model gives us an idea (though a distorted one) of how we would look in those clothes; the Indian village provides us with a picture of the surroundings in which most Indians lived.

Second, models omit some details of the object they represent. These details are usually irrelevant to the purposes of the model. Thus, the concept of the model student will not include details of the student's hair color (although the concept of the model cheerleader may well include such details!). This omission means that the model is usually a simplified version of the other object.

Third, some models have the purpose of *recommending* characteristics of the other object.

In this way, we can arrive at a working definition of a model: it is a way of looking at a real-life object by omitting those aspects that are considered irrelevant and outlining the relationships considered important for present purposes.

If this definition is correct, you can see that we often use models without referring to them as such.

A map is a model because it reproduces only some of the features of a certain area. It may, for example, provide only the information necessary to help one find one's way. Similarly, a dress pattern is a model providing enough information for the dressmaker to be able to make a dress. A designer's sketch is also a model that shows roughly what the dress will look like. Note that while these last two may both be models of the same dress, they give different information. A dressmaker cannot use the designer's sketch directly to make the dress, and one cannot know the appearance of the dress just by looking at the pattern.

This is an important point. Since a model is an abstraction—a simplification of reality—it is possible to have different models of the same piece of reality. The type of model will depend on its intended purpose.

WHAT KINDS OF SIMPLIFICATION ARE USEFUL?

The ship of state; the scales of justice; the winds of change; the Iron Curtain. These ideas are all simplifications of various aspects of society. Strictly speaking, they are not, however, models; they simply do not contain enough information. They are analogies (comparisons), and their use has long been popular for making sense of a complex reality.

Some analogies are merely schematic. The concept of the ship of state cannot be interpreted to mean that all the relationships that exist on board a ship will also be found in a civil state; it can only mean that different groups can be identified by means of the comparison. On the other hand, the English economist Alfred Marshall suggested that business firms grow like "the young trees of the forrest."[1] They start as seedlings, grow slowly to maturity, then decay and die. This analogy of the life cycle of a business firm being like that of a tree is much more like a model. If he was able to identify where the firm was in its cycle, then Marshall felt that he could predict the way in which the firm would be likely to develop over time.

By comparison, the analogy of the ship of state can do very little. It cannot help predict how a particular society will behave, nor can it forecast how the group will develop. It can only suggest that it should be possible to identify social groups analogous to the captain, the crew, the passengers, and so forth. It may also suggest the need for common interests in the community (for example, the general agreement about the purpose of the voyage suggests the need for general agreement about the political objectives of the community). It cannot tell you how this agreement should be reached other than in authoritarian terms.

Although analogies are useful for informal discussions, they cannot by themselves take us very far. They can, however, often form the basis of more formal models by providing clues about the structure of the problem. Therefore, models are often based on an analogy made sometime in the past. For example, many models in economics are based on an analogy with Newtonian physics. This analogy enabled economists to build powerful models of economic equilibria—that is, the positions reached by the economy when all changes have worked themselves out. Thus, economists build models in which price will not change if demand is equal to supply—an obvious analogy with the behavior of a pair of scales.

We have, however, begun to put the cart before the horse by introducing the idea of using models in scientific reasoning before defining the word science. We shall have to backtrack a little in order to examine exactly what a science is.

---

[1] Alfred Marshall, *Principles of Economics*, 8th ed. (London: Macmillan & Co., 1922), p. 315.

Isaac Newton, 1642–1727

Newton was one of the founders of modern physics. One of his most important ideas was that "for every action there is an equal and opposite reaction." Thus, he introduced the idea of forces balancing each other.

WHAT IS A SCIENCE?

A particular science such as physics or chemistry is commonly defined in terms of its subject matter.[2] We can see that such a definition is incomplete by comparing astronomy and astrology. Both studies are concerned with the movement of heavenly bodies, but most people (though not all) would agree that astronomy is a science while astrology is not. What reason do we have for making this distinction?

The fundamental difference is surely that of method. The principal aim of astronomers is to produce statements about the behavior of planets, stars or other celestial objects that can be tested by observation. It can be argued, though, that astrologers also produce statements that could be tested. The crucial difference is that astronomers *do in fact test their statements*, whereas the astrologers are *not themselves concerned with testing*. Another difference connected with this is that, in general, not only do astrologers fail to test their statements, but they also do not usually produce statements capable of being tested. Statements such as: "You will meet a tall, dark stranger who will have an important effect on your life," although seemingly specific, are not unambiguous enough to be tested. *When* will you meet the stranger? *How* tall will he be? *How* dark? What is considered *important*? All of these ambiguities make the testing of the original statement almost totally dependent on the judgment of the tester.

We can now see that the aim of science is to produce general statements that can be tested about the behavior of

---

[2]Thus, physics is defined as "The science of matter and energy and the interaction between the two," and chemistry as "The science of the composition, structure, properties and reactions of matter." (William Morris (ed.), *American Heritage Dictionary of the English Language.* Boston: American Heritage Publishing Co. and Houghton Mifflin Company, 1973.)

certain phenomena. Not only should these statements be *capable* of being tested, but they should also in fact *be* tested.

How do scientists organize their work so that they can arrive at this stage? In general, the techniques depend upon the subject of the science, although all sciences share some similarities. All scientists engage in observation, classification (sorting their observations), prediction (making statements about expected behavior), testing (seeing whether their statements are confirmed by observation), and modification (changing an unsatisfactory model). The differences between sciences manifest themselves not only in the subject of study but also in the way in which observation and testing are carried out. Scientists in some fields (e.g., physics, chemistry, and biology) can carry out their studies in a laboratory under controlled conditions. They can study the phenomenon in which they are interested in isolation without interference from other events. Researchers in other sciences (astronomy, economics) cannot study their subjects under controlled conditions. They have to take them as they are and study their behavior within a vastly more complicated system. In order to do so, they have developed sophisticated techniques to help them isolate the effects of individual factors.

What does all this have to do with models? The answer is "almost everything." Without at least a rudimentary model, the scientist would not know which phenomena he should observe or how he should classify his observations. Without a more sophisticated model, he would not be able to produce predictions or know what factors he should isolate to test them.

The building of models is fundamental to the practice of science. Reality is so complex that we have to use models to guide and illuminate our thinking. The analogies in common use can be thought of as being at one end of a spectrum of transformations of reality that reduce reality to manageable proportions. At the other end of the spectrum are sophisticated mathematical models.

WHAT IS ECONOMICS?

It is all about managing your money! It is about managing the economy! It is about making money on the stock market! It is about getting things cheaply!

Although none of these popular definitions of economics really gets to the heart of the matter, they do contain some elements of truth. Essentially, economics is the "science which studies human behavior as a relationship between ends and scarce means which have alternative uses."[3] The decision about how to allocate scarce means to achieve certain ends can be made by an individual, a family, or a government. Economic theory is interested in situations in which a decision maker who would like to have more of two different things can only have more of one thing by giving up the other. So economics can be concerned with such issues as the decision of an individual to buy steak rather than a theater ticket; the decision of a family to buy a larger house and postpone indefinitely the purchase of a second automobile; or the decision of a government to allocate more money to defense and less to education.

FOOD FOR THOUGHT

Are models useful to economists? What kinds of models do economists use? How do they set about building them? The following chapters will try to answer these questions.

Chapter 2 is concerned with the first stages of model-building: observation and classification. It discusses the problems encountered during these stages and how they can be solved. Chapter 3 discusses how observation and classification may be used to formulate questions. What determines the type of question? How are the questions formulated? Chapter 4 deals with the different types of answers, in particular with the kinds of answers (i.e., models) used by economists. Chapter 5 looks at the problems connected with the use of models. Are models useful for economists? What are the pitfalls to be avoided in using them? Chapter 6 is concerned with testing. How do we know whether we have a good model? What kinds of changes would improve an unsatisfactory model? Chapter 7 discusses the choice of language in which models are written and also gives some useful mathematical techniques. The discussion of statistics in Chapter 8 provides some tools that are used in the testing of

---

[3]Lionel Robbins, *An Essay on the Nature and Significance of Economic Science*, 2nd Edition. (London: Macmillan & Co., 1935.) Although this definition is quite old, it is still accepted implicitly by most modern economists.

models. So Chapters 2 through 8 are essentially about the five stages of model-building: observation, classification, prediction, testing, and modification. While it is useful to discuss the modeling process in these stages, the actual procedure is more complex than this and it tends to be circular. Modification leads to new observations and perhaps to new classifications. Observation itself necessitates the formation of some rudimentary classifications, which may be refined in the light of new observations. Because of this circularity, some important points appear under different guises in more than one chapter. Bear with us on this repetition. It is a result of the nature of the subject and not of the rambling of economists who do not know when to stop.

Now read on!

QUESTIONS

1. What different types of models can you now identify? What are their common features?

2. In what ways is an artist's model like other models? In what respects does it differ from other models? Are these differences important?

3. Models of a particular class of objects can be used as a basis for comparison. For example, the model of an Indian village is systematic and standardized, but because each particular village was constructed in a different geographical location, it is likely to be a modified version of the standardized model. How can such a model help us to understand the causes and significance of these modifications?

4. We often hear people say, "But that is a false analogy." What is an analogy? When is it legitimate to use one?

5. What is meant by scientific method? On what grounds could you argue that economics is a science while astrology is not?

DESCRIPTION

2

Let these describe the undescribable.

— Lord Byron

... Chicago is a great American city. ... [it] grew up from the savory of its neighborhoods to some of the best high-rise architecture in the world, and because its people were Poles and Ukrainians and Czechs as well as Irish and the rest, the city had Byzantine corners worthy of Prague or Moscow, odd tortured attractive drawbridges over the Chicago River, huge Gothic spires like the skyscrapers which held the Chicago Tribune, curves and abutments and balconies in cylindrical structures thirty stories high twisting in and out of the curves of the river, and fine balustrades in its parks. ...

... To the West of the Lake were factories and Ciceros, Mafialands and immigrant lands: to the North, the suburbs, the Evanstons; to the South were Negro ghettos of the South Side — belts of Black men, amplifying each the resonance of the other's cause — the Black belt had the Blackstone Rangers, the largest gang of juvenile delinquents on earth, 2,000 by some count — one could be certain the gang had leaders as large in potential as Hannibal or Attila the Hun — how else account for the strength and wit of a stud who would try to rise so high in the Blackstone Rangers.

Further South and West were enclaves for the University of Chicago, more factories, more neighborhoods for Poles, some measure of more good hotels on the lake, and endless neighborhoods — white neighborhoods which went for miles of ubiquitous dingy wood houses with back yards, neighborhoods to hint of Eastern Europe, Ireland, Tennessee, a gathering of all the clans of the Midwest, the Indians, and Scotch-Irish, Swedes, some Germans, Italians, Hungarians, Rumanians, Finns, Slovaks, Slovenes — it was only the French who did not travel. In the Midwest, land spread out; not five miles from the Loop were areas as empty, deserted, enormous and mournful by night as the outer freight yards of Omaha. Some industrial desert or marsh would lie low on the horizon, an area squalling by day, deserted by night, except for the hulking Midwestern names of the boxcars and the low sheds, the warehouse buildings, the wire fences which went along the side of unpaved roads for thousands of yards. ...[1]

Norman Mailer's description re-creates the atmosphere of a large, vibrant city. Table 1 gives precise information about certain features of the city, such as the size of its population,

[1]From MIAMI AND THE SIEGE OF CHICAGO by Norman Mailer. Copyright © 1968 by Norman Mailer. By arrangement with The New American Library, Inc., New York, N.Y.

TABLE 1. Selected Statistics of Chicago, 1970

Total population	3,367,000
Land area (sq. miles)	222.6
Population per sq. mile	15,126
Suspended particulate matter[1]	
(micrograms per cu. m.)[2]	145
Mean number of days for which the	
minimum temperature was 32°F or less	119
Normal monthly average temperature (°F)	
January	26.0
February	27.7
March	36.3
April	49.0
May	60.0
June	70.5
July	75.6
August	74.3
September	66.4
October	55.3
November	39.7
December	29.1

From U.S. Bureau of the Census, *Statistical Abstract of the United States.*

[1]Particles of smoke, dust, fumes, and droplets of viscous liquid remaining in the air for varying periods of time and ranging from less than 1 micron (1/25,000 inch) to 100 microns in diameter.

[2]Arithmetic average, 1969.

the extent of its land area, its weather, and so forth. Figure 2.1 shows the spatial relationships between one part of the city and another, while Figure 2.2 gives us some idea of how the city would look if we were standing on the spot from which the photograph was taken.

There are, of course, many other methods of describing a city. It could be represented by a piece of music, by a poem, by a scale model, or by a painting. You might like to consider, for example, the types of descriptions given in a song such as *Chicago.* The only common feature of these different descriptions seems to be the piece of reality that they are describing.

It is clear that all of these descriptions omit some details of the city. Mailer's description provides some rudimentary information about the spatial relationships within the city, but he omits so much detail of these relationships that his would not be a useful description for a stranger who wishes to find the way to a specific street. Yet it would be useful to a stranger who wanted to know something about the atmosphere of the city. Conversely, the map can tell us very little

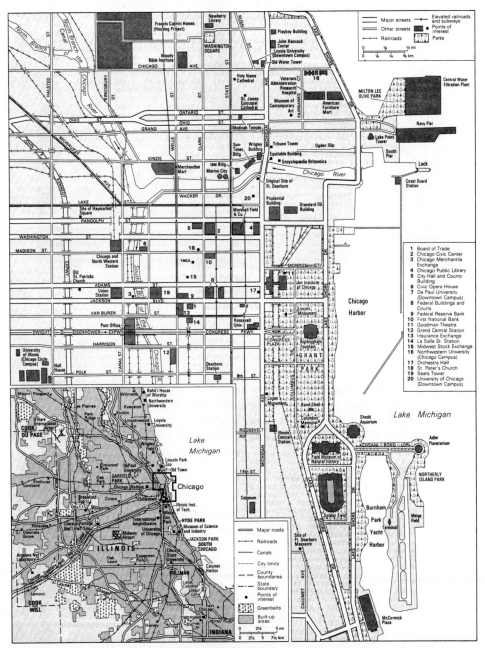

Figure 2–1. Map of Chicago. (Reprinted with permission from *Encyclopaedia Britannica*, 15th edition, © 1974 by Encyclopaedia Britannica, Inc.)

Figure 2-2. High in the sky.

about what the city actually looks like, but it would be extremely useful in helping us to plot a route through the city. Such points are true of all descriptions. Their omissions make them useless or, at best, not very useful, for purposes for which they were not intended.

If all these descriptions of the city of Chicago omit so many details, can they be accurate? Indeed, what is or would be an accurate description? Would it be one that includes all the details of the original? What kind of description would that be?

There is a passage by Lewis Carroll that gives an account of such a complete description:

"What do you consider the *largest* map that would be really useful?"

"About six inches to the mile."

"About *six inches*!" exclaimed Mein Herr. "We very soon got six *yards* to the mile. And then came the grandest idea of all! We actually made a map of the country on the scale of a *mile to a mile*!"

"Have you used it much?" I enquired.

"It has never been spread out yet," said Mein Herr. "The farmers objected. They said it would cover the whole country and shut out the sunlight!"[2]

Moreover, Mein Herr wanted to include only those details in the two-dimensional plane! He did not intend to show the shapes and the sizes of the houses in his country or the shapes and the sizes of the people. Obviously, an attempt to include all details in one description would result in the reduplication of the original subject; this is neither practical nor desirable.

Descriptions are produced to answer implicit questions such as, "What is Chicago like?" In its normal context, this question usually means, "What are the striking features of the city of Chicago?" That is, the questioner wants to learn something of the essence of Chicago. He does not want to be bombarded with billions of details. He wants to obtain an outline of the city and will usually choose to examine the one that gives him the kind of information in which he is most interested. Perhaps he will choose several different outlines or descriptions so that he can try to integrate several sets of information.

The creator of a description is in a similar situation. He is interested in certain features of the city and wishes to communicate them. He is not saying that other aspects do not exist, but rather that he is not interested in them at the present time.

This necessarily results in distortion. It is a distortion caused not by an inability to tell the truth, but by an inability to tell the *whole* truth. Do we then have to accept a distorted view of the real world?

DISTORTION BY OMISSION

What details are omitted from a description? How does the maker of the description decide on the details to be included? Does he have any systematic reasons for his omissions, or are they made on a random basis? What effects do omissions have on the users of descriptions?

---

[2]Lewis Carroll, *Sylvie and Bruno Concluded.* (London: Macmillan & Co., 1889.)

The reasons for and the effects of these omissions depend on the type of omission. There are broadly two types: voluntary and involuntary.[3] Although they are interdependent, they can for the most part be treated separately.

Details are omitted voluntarily for four reasons. First, they may be omitted because their inclusion would obscure features that the author considers more important. They are left out to simplify the description and to make it more effective. Second, they may be omitted because neither the author nor his audience is interested in them. Third, they may not be included because the author assumes that his audience already has information that will allow them to obtain these details themselves. Finally, they may be omitted with the deliberate intention of deceiving the audience.

The first and second types of omission are related. The cartographer usually omits details about the size and the style of buildings in the city, because he and his audience are only concerned with obtaining a plan of the city with which they can plot a route from one place to another. He omits these details both because he is not interested in them and because he wishes to make the map more portable and easier to read. These omissions are of both the first and second types.

The user of this map will probably be interested in how long his journey is going to take. The map does not include this information because many factors other than just mileage are involved. In addition to the information contained in the map, the user will need information about the method of transportation and about possible delays. The additional information he requires can be obtained more easily from other sources. These omissions are of the third type.

A map might include the route of a new highway but fail to mention that it is still under construction and is thus not yet in use. This omission might be intended to convey the idea that the area is more advanced economically than is in fact the case. Omissions of this fourth type are obviously fraudulent. Although they may be extremely useful for the

---

[3]Although all these types of omission also occur in the building of economic models, this chapter will be concerned only with their general effects on description. The effects on economic models will be discussed in Chapter 5.

purposes of their author, they are very misleading to the audience. On the other hand, omissions of the first three types are intended to help the audience. Because omissions from the map make it more portable and easier to read, they make the description more efficient. It therefore fulfills its purpose more effectively.

Involuntary omissions occur for two reasons. First, the medium chosen by the author may not communicate certain details. A photograph cannot communicate the sounds of the city, while a table of statistics cannot communicate the city's visual appearance. The author *can,* however, choose his medium; these involuntary omissions are likely to be a result of the pattern of his interests.

Second, details may be involuntarily omitted because the author is not aware of them. If he had noticed that these details were missing, he would have included them. Such an omission is a result of a failure in perception — a rich and fascinating subject.

It may be useful to end this section with a summary of the types of omissions that occur during the process of description.

A. Voluntary
  1. Simplification
  2. Lack of interest
  3. Information assumed to be available elsewhere in a more convenient form
  4. Misleading the audience

B. Involuntary
  1. Limitations of the medium
  2. Limitations in perception

Some distortions, of course, give us more cause for concern than do others. Types A.4 and B.2 are particularly serious because they directly mislead the audience. The other types of omission will only mislead an audience that is not aware of the author's purpose: that is, these omissions will result in serious distortion only if the expectations of the author differ from those of his audience.

The next section of this chapter is concerned with the distortions caused by limitations in perception. We are devoting an entire section to this type of omission (B.2) not necessarily because it is the most important, but because it is less obvious than the others.

DISTORTION AND PERCEPTION

How far can we trust our own judgment? Can we indeed believe our eyes? How dangerous are preconceived ideas to the practice of science?

Description and its accompanying activities of simplification and classification depend for their effectiveness on accurate observation. To some extent we see only what we expect to see. This cliché does not mean that we *know* what we are going to see, but that we approach each experience with a particular "mental set" that makes it possible to interpret the experience. A mental set is a way of looking at the world in the light of previous experience which enables us to make sense of what we see and hear. It is, in a sense, a rudimentary model of the world which helps us to interpret our experiences.

Problems can arise when we have a choice of mental sets, however. A simple example will illustrate this point. Is the sketch in Figure 2.3 a drawing of a duck or of a rabbit? If you look at it in one way, you will see a duck. If you look at it in another way, the beak will become ears and you will see a rabbit. It is impossible to see both the duck and the rabbit at the same time. It is relatively easy to switch quite quickly from one interpretation to the other and to remember while seeing one that the other is possible. You cannot see both at once, however.

How is this relevant to the process of description? A

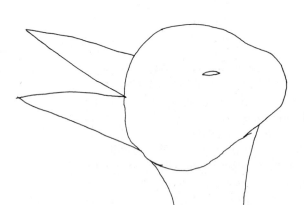

Figure 2–3. Duck or rabbit?

group of medical students were shown X-rays of two hands.[4] The students were asked to describe these hands. It became clear that they used a great amount of prior knowledge and experience—a certain mental set—in making their descriptions. For example, they made statements such as "A is a young hand and B is an old hand." This is not a description of what exists in the photograph but is a statement of what the students "saw" as a result of their knowledge of X-rays and human anatomy.

Less striking examples may be given. An English person describing Chicago would almost certainly mention the regular, symmetrical pattern of its streets. In most English cities and towns, streets are of different lengths and form irregular patterns. The experience of visiting a city in which all the streets run either north to south or east to west would be so unique that it would be worth mentioning. Norman Mailer *knows* that the streets follow this regular pattern, but he is not *aware* of it while making his description. He is in the situation of seeing the rabbit while knowing that a duck could also be seen.

In many cases such as the latter, the author chooses his mental set at the same time as he chooses his interests. Omissions made in this way are not involuntary. If one is not aware of the existence of possible alternatives, however, serious distortions can result.

Consider a hypothetical description of the academic performance of a class of children. One possible description might be:

The average math score in the class was 65%. The average math score among the boys was 66%, and the average score among the girls was 64%. On the average, the boys had better scores than the girls.

This description is the result of a mental set that sees the class as two groups: a group of boys and a group of girls. It could be considered acceptable because the scores seem to support this grouping, although the difference between the groups is very small. We should be careful not to conclude from this that this is the only (or even the most appropriate) way of looking at the problem.

---

[4]Quoted by M. L. Abercrombie Johnson, *The Anatomy of Judgement: Investigation into the Processes of Perception and Reasoning.* (Harmondsworth: Penguin Books Ltd., 1969.)

An imaginative researcher might develop another mental set and produce this description:

The average math score of the class was 65%. The children with above average sized feet achieved a score of 70%, and those with below average sized feet scored 60%. Children with big feet obtained better scores than those with small feet.

This description uses two groups that differ from each other more than the groups in the first description do. A different mental set is required to "see" these two new groups. This hypothetical example makes several points.

First, it illustrates the importance of avoiding complacence with existing mental sets. In our example, one who was satisfied with the first description would have identified girls as a group that had more difficulty with mathematics than did boys. With the introduction of the second description, however, it seems reasonable to shift attention to another group of children—those with small feet.

Second, the example illustrates the danger of natural classifications. Both classifications are natural in the sense that the groups are defined by characteristics determined at birth. Yet are both categories as fundamental as the male/female classification is often thought to be? Indeed, in our example, the classification "big feet/small feet" produced greater differences in academic performance, but it is unlikely that anyone would claim that this is a fundamental classification to be used for all purposes. It seems more useful for us to choose the characteristics of groups that provide a useful classification for our immediate purpose and to remain open to the possibility of other useful classifications existing.

Can we go further and say that there are no natural categories? What, after all, do we mean by natural? Discussions of natural categories often seem to imply that there is some kind of heavenly filing system underlying classifications which it is the job of scientists to discover.

We do not believe that it is useful to search for classifications of this sort. It seems more useful for us to be flexible and to use different classifications for different purposes. For example, an eagle may be placed either in the category "predators" or in the category "birds." Which is the more natural category? Does it even matter? The category chosen should depend on one's purpose. Are we comparing the eating habits of different species, or are we comparing birds to other animals?

Similarly, economics takes the individual person as the basic entity and places each individual into categories such as Producers, Consumers, or Laborers. Again, one person could belong to more than one category. Each person usually belongs to at least two categories — Consumers and some type of Producer. In the Robinson Crusoe economy, Crusoe belonged to all categories.

Indeed, it can even be a hindrance for a science to treat all categories as natural. Keynesian economics influenced countries to gather statistics based on Keynesian categories. Thus, all expenditures were forced into classifications corresponding to the Keynesian concepts of Consumption and Investment. Later work, because of the form in which data were available, was sometimes forced into the Keynesian mold. Work that took the point of view that different types of expenditures depend on relative prices and that therefore made no sharp distinction between consumption and investment was hindered because of the lack of suitable data.

Our hypothetical example of the academic performance of a class of children makes a third point. The mental set with which a description is undertaken will depend to some extent on the values of the observer. A person who believes that men and women should play different roles is more likely to "see" the class as a group of boys and a group of girls than a person who does not hold this belief.

This section started by saying that one sees what one expects to see; it is now saying that one expects to see what one wants to see. This does not, however, mean that values necessarily block perception; an awareness of these limitations can enable one to search positively to acquire new mental sets. Perception will still be limited, but it will be expanding and will be capable of even further expansion. Moreover, as perception expands, it is possible for one's value system to change also. The person who believes that male and female roles are different and immutable may change his mind as his mental set expands to include other classifications. Therefore, the responsible scientist should be aware of the possibility of the existence of classifications other than those that he is currently using, and he should be prepared to consider alternative ways of looking at his subject.

QUESTIONS

1. Describe in five or six sentences the impression of Chicago that you have gained from Mailer's passage.

2. Compare the table of statistics of Chicago with the salient features of Mailer's description. Answer the following questions.

    (a) Do they have any data in common?
    (b) Which set of data provides the most effective description?
    (c) If you were a sociologist attempting to investigate gang organization in Chicago, what sort of quantifiable information would you use to replace Mailer's qualitative information?

3. Description is frequently the first stage in the modeling process. What are the features of a description? What kinds of distortions are there in descriptions because of the media used to convey them?

4. List the types of omissions that occur during the production of a description.

5. If we thought that ethnic groupings were important to the development of social and political life in Chicago, what kind of quantitative data would we present to prove the importance of these groups?

6. What is meant by *mental set*? What do you think is meant by *normal vision*?

QUESTIONS AND ANSWERS $\quad$ **3**

Questioning is not the mode of conversation among gentlemen.
— Dr. Johnson

What is the relationship between questions and answers? What indeed is a question, and why do we ask it? How are questions formed, and which are important? What kinds of questions are there?

Model-building can be viewed as a process of forming fairly rigorous and carefully constructed answers to certain often implicit questions. Most of this book discusses the construction and the validity of such answers, but in this chapter the emphasis will be on questions. The relationship between questions and answers is so close that it is difficult to discuss them separately. To a great extent, the form of the question predetermines the answer; this is a problem that continuously gives trouble to model-builders. Conversely, an answer of any sort implies a question of a given type. For example, the previous chapter was a discussion of the validity of answers to one sort of question. Description is an answer to the relatively simple question, "What is it like?" As we have seen, even the answers to such relatively simple questions create difficulties. The answers to more complex questions are even more problematic.

WHAT IS A QUESTION?

Sometimes questions are so ambiguous—perhaps because they are poorly expressed—that it may be difficult to recognize them as such. In spite of this occasional ambiguity, we can all usually recognize a question when we hear one. It is, of course, a request for information and is therefore connected intimately with its answer.

Since science is concerned with the acquisition of information, the formulation of questions and the development of their answers is the principal activity of science. Scientists have to know how to ask questions to accumulate knowledge of their subject. Yet not all questions are of interest to scientists. It is important for them to be able to distinguish between those questions that are answerable and those that are not.

Answerable questions are the subject of scientific inquiry. This does not mean that the answers are obvious, for if they were, there would be nothing for scientists to do. It simply means that present techniques can be used to search for an answer to such questions.

Questions without answers should not necessarily be ignored by scientists. It may be possible to rephrase an unanswerable question to obtain one that can be answered. Why does God allow poverty and starvation to persist? This is not an answerable question for a scientist, although theologians may offer some answers. The question could, however, be rephrased as "What are the causes of poverty and starvation?" Now *this* question could have a scientific answer. The difference between the theological answers to the first question and the possible scientific answers to the second is, of course, the existence of the possibility of appealing to evidence. With present techniques, the theologians cannot settle their differences by appealing to evidence; the scientists, however, can. Indeed, it could be argued that theology, to some extent, and philosophy, to a far greater extent, are not sciences precisely because they are not really interested in obtaining answers. They are, rather, more interested in the proper phrasing of questions.

How does one recognize unanswerable questions? After all, if the scientist is engaged in finding answers that are not immediately obvious, how can he tell whether an answer is possible at all?

This is part of a scientist's skill. It requires a delicate interaction between judgment and knowledge: knowledge about the existing answers and about the techniques and evidence available; judgment about the way in which the boundaries of this knowledge may be expanded. It is this interaction between knowledge and judgment that must be a recurring theme in any discussion of model-building.

The Double Helix
An Exercise in Skill and Judgment

B. Crick and J. D. Watson are the two bio-
chemists who discovered the chemical
structure of DNA—the basic genetic code.
They needed both the knowledge of the relevant areas of biology and chemistry, and
the judgment to see that they could "crack
the code" with the existing knowledge. Watson tells the fascinating story of their discovery in *The Double Helix.*

WHY ARE QUESTIONS ASKED?

The simple pursuit of knowledge prompts many questions. People want to know about the world around them. The
child's question, "How are cakes made?," is really the same
type of question as the physicist's when he asks, "What is the
structure of the atom?" Both the child and the physicist want
the information for its own sake.

The other reason for seeking information is to learn how
to change the world in some way. The answers to such questions obviously have to include some information about the
way in which the world actually works. It would be madness
to try to build a nuclear power station (which tries under
special conditions to change the structure of certain atoms to
produce energy) without knowing a good deal about the
structure and the behavior of the atom under different conditions. This may seem so obvious as to be hardly worth saying.

In connection with this, however, one should consider the
way in which economic policy is carried out: Taxes are increased or decreased; public expenditure is manipulated;
wages or prices, or both, are frozen. All this is undertaken
with very little knowledge about the effects of such measures
on national income, the level of employment, the rate of inflation, and so forth.

HOW ARE QUESTIONS FORMED?

Sometimes the world around us forces us to ask certain
questions. The Great Depression probably had a great influ-

ence on Keynes' development of the question, "Why does large-scale unemployment persist?" The Second World War probably had some impact on the question, "How can the atom be split?"

This influence can be overstated, however. Keynes needed some imagination to identify the problem as one of *persistent* unemployment. The possibility of splitting the atom existed before the Second World War; it followed from Einstein's revolutionary view of light as bundles of energy instead of a stream. Scientists engage in an imaginative creative process to develop new questions and to seek their answers.

Imagination is a valuable attribute for a scientist and is essentially the same quality as that possessed by an artist. It is the ability to create something new: new images, new ideas, new questions, new categories. With imagination, people are able to transcend the existing view of the world and to see it in a new light. This ability gives rise to great works of art like Picasso's *Guernica*—a style of painting that produced a new view of the agonies of war—and to important scientific research such as Keynes' *General Theory*—a new way of looking at the economic system.

John Maynard Keynes

J. M. Keynes was a prolific writer on economics whose best-known work, *The General Theory of Employment, Interest and Money*, affected the economic policies of governments for many years. Economists before Keynes had treated unemployment as a temporary phenomenon that would disappear if the labor market was left alone. That is, they had essentially been asking the question, "*What* economic mechanism insures full employment?" Keynes asked the revolutionary question, "Suppose that unemployment is not temporary—what causes it to persist? Thus, his question was, "*Is there* an economic mechanism that insures full employment?" He also introduced many other innovations into economic theory.

One may dispute Keynes' theoretical structure, but one can hardly dispute either his impact, both on policy and on the thinking of economists, or his imaginative flair.

WHAT KINDS OF QUESTIONS ARE THERE?

What is it like? What causes it? What would happen if . . . ? What would be best?

These four questions summarize the main types that can be asked, and they correspond to four main types of answers. The first question asks for a description and the second for an explanation, while the third asks for a prediction. There are, of course, many subdivisions within these main categories.

The fourth question cuts across the other three, since it is a question about the best of all possible situations. Such questions are called *normative questions* and should be clearly distinguished from questions of the first three types, which are called *positive questions*. Normative questions are not scientific, since the answers to them depend upon value judgments and not upon appeal to the facts of the real world.

All these different types of questions and answers are the subject of the next chapter. Although all types of questions are important, those actually asked depend on many different factors: the imagination of the questioner, the present state of knowledge, and the demands of policy.

ASKING THE RIGHT QUESTION

Questions are important because to some extent they predetermine the answers by making some impossible. "How is the demand for meat affected by changes in income?" may be an interesting question. If the demand for meat is more responsive to changes in price than to changes in income, however, this question may not be very useful for the development of agricultural policy. "Is total consumption expenditure related to national income?" precludes the consideration of categories other than "consumption expenditure" and "national income."

Therefore, to obtain useful answers and consequently powerful models, we have to be able to formulate useful questions. This process is seldom explicit, and it demands judgment, imagination, and flexibility. Good judgment enables one to identify a problem area revealed either by the environment (the Depression, the Second World War) or by inconsistencies with existing theories that show up in experimental results. Imagination is the means by which one is able to begin to formulate useful questions—and their answers. Finally, flexibility is almost the most important of all;

it is the ability to spot the red herring, to turn back from a fruitless path of research, and to have the courage to start to ask new questions again.

QUESTIONS

1. What is a question? Review the reasons why the form of a question might help to predetermine the answer.

2. Reformulate, if possible, the following questions into statements that can be scientifically investigated, given current techniques:

   (a) Why does God allow famine to exist?
   (b) Why did God create the universe?
   (c) What should the distribution of income be?
   (d) Why are the Rain Gods on high mountains more powerful than the Rain Gods on low hills?

3. What are the various reasons for asking questions?

4. Consider the two questions below. Tell how they differ and how you think the answers to them would differ:

   Why has the automatic stabilizing mechanism failed to produce full employment?
   Is there an automatic stabilizing mechanism?

5. Keynes and Malthus both looked at economic slumps and their consequences. Both came up with similar conclusions about effective demand. Does this mean that economic questions are historically determined?

6. What are the different types of questions that you are likely to encounter in the social sciences?

TYPES OF MODELS AND THEIR FUNCTIONS

4

Rules and models destroy genius and art.

—William Hazlitt

What is it like? What causes it? What would happen if...? What would be best? Science is concerned with finding answers to the first three questions, and scientists build models to obtain these answers. As a part of this activity, scientists also build models whose primary purpose cannot be so neatly determined by a simple question. These models aim to improve the understanding of the subject. They do not in themselves provide answers, but they may lead to models that do. So we can say that various *scientific* models attempt to fulfill four functions: description, prediction, explanation, and understanding. Models that try to answer the fourth type of question, "What would be best?," are attempts to express the characteristics of a desirable state of the world. We shall see that such questions are not scientific because their answers cannot be tested by an appeal to the facts of the real world.

Models that describe are perhaps the easiest ones to build, but even this process is not completely straightforward. Although Chapter 2 was devoted to this subject, it could do little more than scratch the surface of many difficult problems. Many of the problems that occur in making a description are common to all forms of model-building. In particular, the choice of classification and the problems of distortion should be borne in mind when building models of any kind.

Most discussions of models (particularly of those used in

the social sciences) will classify them into one or more of the basic classifications of description, prediction, explanation, and understanding.

POSITIVE AND NORMATIVE

This is a basic distinction in economic theory. It can also be relevant to models in other sciences—particularly in other social sciences—but the distinction has been of special importance in economics.

In principle, positive analysis is concerned with what *is* and tries to establish the relationships that exist in the real world. Positive statements can therefore be tested by the observation of the real world. Normative analysis is concerned with what *should be* and cannot be tested by an appeal to the facts. One cannot make an *incorrect* normative statement because all normative statements depend only upon personal values. Of course, if a normative statement is derived by logical reasoning from certain values that are considered "basic," then if the reasoning is faulty, one may argue that the statement is not "logical." But one cannot argue that it does not conform with what he observes and is therefore wrong, because normative statements are intended not to reflect the *real* world but to express the characteristics of an *ideal* world. Thus, normative statements never yield predictions that can be observed and validated in the real world. Positive statements *can* yield such predictions.

Yet if we are interested in making social policy, we have to be able to make both positive and normative statements. We also have to know which kind of statement we are making at each stage in the analysis. Figure 4.1 shows the basic relationships between positive and normative statements and the resulting policy action. Positive analysis of the situation provides predictions about the outcomes of various actions, while normative analysis results in a statement of the desirability of different outcomes. The policy decision is formulated after both these analyses have been completed even though, they are, of course, not often undertaken explicitly. The decision itself is a result of both the normative analysis, which determines the desired outcome, and the positive analysis, which provides information about the way in which this outcome can be achieved. Confusion sometimes arises from an inability to understand and disentangle these very different activities.

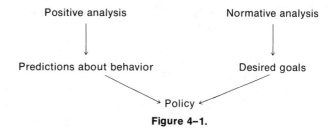

Figure 4–1.

As an example of the distinction between positive and normative statements in economic policy, consider the debate about unemployment and inflation. A model that has been very popular in recent years predicts a relationship between inflation and unemployment such that an increase in the level of unemployment will decrease the rate of inflation. (This relationship is called the Phillips' curve, named after A. W. Phillips, who first observed it.[1]) The statement of the existence of this relationship is a positive statement that can be tested by examining the behavior of the rates of inflation and of unemployment in the past.[2] On the other hand, the statement, "The government should increase the level of unemployment because this will slow the rate of inflation," contains the normative judgment that it is better to have unemployment than inflation. You may disagree with this normative judgment on ethical grounds, but you cannot *disprove* it. If you could, the statement would be a positive one resulting from some other model of behavior. Ultimately, however, you have to make some value judgments, because to make policy one has to choose between various states of the world. This choice involves normative judgments about which state is better. You cannot avoid this choice by building bigger and better models or by hiding your values in the model itself. At some point, you have to decide what you think is right and what is wrong. It is much better to make these value judgments explicitly.[3]

---

[1] A. W. Phillips, "The Relationship between Unemployment and the Rate of Change of Money Wage Rates in the United Kingdom, 1861–1957." *Economica*, Vol. 25 (November 1958), pp. 283–299.

[2] This positive statement has been refuted by more recent evidence. It is still a positive statement, however. Positive statements can be wrong! Although they may be illogical, normative statements can never be wrong.

[3] This last sentence was not intended to be a normative statement. It is really a positive statement meaning, "It is *more efficient* from the point of view of policy-making to make these value judgments explicitly." Note that not all statements containing "better," "best," or "worse" are normative.

At a simple level, it seems quite easy to distinguish between normative and positive statements. When pushed to its limits, however, the distinction becomes a little fuzzy. For example, when we speak of a "normal" person, we are making a positive statement about the way in which most people behave.[4] Yet this phrase also has a normative content, since we often think that it is good to be normal and bad to be abnormal. So if we say that a certain person is not normal, we are usually making both a positive and a normative statement. The positive statement is that this person does not act in the same way that most other people do; the normative implication is that it would be better if he did.

The distinction between positive and normative statements becomes still more blurred when one examines many normative statements more closely. "It is good to be normal" is apparently a normative statement of one's opinion. If pressed, however, the speaker may justify this statement by claiming that normal people are better equipped to cope with the strains of everyday life. Now we have a positive statement that can be tested.

Positive and normative aspects are also interrelated in policy decisions. Figure 4.1 showed part of this relationship, but Figure 4.2 shows its more problematic features. We now see that the subjects of positive analysis—that is, the questions to be answered—are determined by normative judgments about their importance and by the demands of the policy field. For example, if unemployment became very widespread, it would be difficult to ignore it. Because of its importance to economic policy, it would become one of the subjects of positive analysis. It is also very likely that it would affect normative judgments about the importance of the subject. Thus, although we have drawn these relationships as though their effects were acting in only one direction, we can now see that the arrows show only the direction of their most common effect. Some can also operate in the opposite direction.[5]

---

[4] A "normal" person is one who behaves in a way similar to that of most other people: that is, his behavior does not deviate greatly from that of the people around him. This phrase also has statistical connotations. The "normal curve" represents a distribution in which most observations are clustered around a central point, with fewer at each extreme. (see Chapter 8.) The everyday use of "normal" is obviously related to this concept.

[5] Figures 4.1 and 4.2 are themselves models. They are descriptive models that outline the important relationships implicit in the positive/normative distinction. Note that they are not flow charts. Much of the interaction takes place simultaneously.

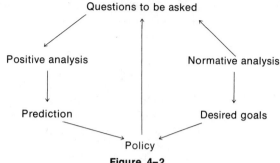

Figure 4–2.

One of the most common models used in economic theory is the model of perfect competition. It is a controversial and much criticized model. Much of this criticism has stemmed from a misunderstanding of the purposes of the model. It can be used in three ways:

Type I: as a description of a particular market—e.g., the wheat market.

Type II: as an analytical tool to predict behavior in a particular market—e.g., the effects of an increased tax on the tobacco market.

Type III: as a prescription about the optimal behavior of a particular market—e.g., the need for antitrust legislation.

The first use is positive and produces a model to describe the characteristics of certain markets. A list of characteristics that describe a perfectly competitive market would include the following:[6]

1. Many sellers
2. Many buyers
3. Homogeneous products
4. Perfect knowledge about prices and costs
5. Perfect mobility of factors
6. Perfect mobility of products
7. Profit maximization
8. Utility maximization
9. Identical costs for all producers

These are the most important criteria used to classify and, therefore, to describe, markets that are perfectly competitive. The markets for most agricultural products will fit this description.

---

[6]Although this list is the one most often seen in introductory texts, it is not strictly accurate. Conditions *1* and *2*, strictly speaking, refer to *potential* sellers and buyers, not to the *actual* numbers engaged in the market.

The second use of the model of perfect competition is also positive. It is used to predict the behavior in markets such as grocery retailing for which all the descriptive characteristics of a perfectly competitive market may not apply, yet the analysis can still yield adequate predictions because the discrepancies do not greatly affect the behavior in which we are interested. Thus, some of the predictions of perfect competition can be validated in markets which do not conform with all the conditions just listed. We can obtain the same predictions with a much shorter list.[7]

The third use of this model is normative. It is employed to show some of the conditions under which the free market will result in an *optimal* allocation of resources. Its usefulness for this purpose depends also on whether the descriptive model is an accurate description of the market concerned. So we can see that there is some connection between the three uses of this model. In many cases, we need to use only the predictive model; thus the market has to fulfill less stringent conditions than those just listed. There are, however, two good reasons for bearing in mind the longer list of characteristics of the descriptive model.

First, there may be situations in which the model fails to predict adequately. In these cases, the longer list acts as a check and may give some information about whether the model of these situations should be modified. Second, the longer list describes a market structure that achieves an optimal allocation of resources in the economy; that is, it provides a normative model. One cannot, however, use the predictive model for normative purposes. It is not satisfactory to say, "This market behaves in a way predicted by the model of perfect competition; therefore, it *is* perfectly competitive and is achieving an optimal allocation of resources." This interpretation of a predictive model as being descriptively accurate is invalid.

There is another more difficult problem that accompanies the distinction between positive and normative statements. Since we cannot grasp reality directly but are depend-

---

[7]It is impossible to provide a shorter list at this stage in your studies without being ambiguous, but it is possible to give an example of one. Products may not be completely homogeneous—the same brand of detergent bought at a store closer to your home is a slightly different product from that bought at a store further away—but they may be such close substitutes that the model of perfect competition may give adequate predictions. Thus, for certain problems, industries can be analyzed *as if* they were perfectly competitive without *in fact* being perfectly competitive.

ent upon our *perception* of it, the facts against which we test our positive statements are chosen according to our perception of them. Our perception depends in turn on our values; and so our distinction between positive and normative breaks down to some extent. This interdependence may not be too serious, however. We have all experienced times when our preconceived ideas were proved wrong. Perception does not depend *entirely* on opinions.

These reservations cause some difficulties in interpreting positive and normative statements. Yet, there are still a wide range of statements that we can safely characterize as either positive or normative. Indeed, we must make the distinction to develop powerful economic theory or to engage in effective economic policy. We can say that most inquiry in the social sciences is concerned with the way in which people *do* behave and with the ways in which their societies *are* organized, and that such inquiry often has the purpose of improving these societies.

PARTIAL/GENERAL, DYNAMIC/STATIC, EQUILIBRIUM/DISEQUILIBRIUM, MICRO/MACRO

Like the positive/normative dichotomy, these alternatives are not as simple as they appear to be at first. Not only is there some confusion in the literature concerning these alternative classifications, but as we shall show, there can also be considerable overlap among them.

Partial/General

The difference between partial and general models is, roughly, a difference in the number of variables in the model. A preliminary way of thinking about general models is that they have a greater number of variables than partial models. There is, however, no magic number of variables at which a partial model becomes a general one. Perhaps an example would help to illustrate the difference more clearly than a definition could alone. A model of a fish market that considered only the price and the quantity of fish, the incomes of fish consumers, the costs to the fishermen, and other variables directly related to the fish market would be a partial model. A model that also included behavior in the meat market would be more general. A model that included the behavior of all the markets in the economy would be still more general.

Since the world is so complex, and since there are many interrelationships between markets, some may argue that general models would be more useful and that partial models may be totally inadequate to deal with the problems we face. Before we accept this wholeheartedly, we should remember the experience of Lewis Carroll's character who included more and more detail in his model until it became completely useless.

A more precise distinction between partial and general models is the number of variables that are excluded from the model. We can say that partial models have a greater number of variables in the category of "ceteris paribus." The use of "ceteris paribus" does not mean that we believe that other things do remain unchanged; it simply means that we believe that the effect of the changes is small. How small is small? The answer really depends on the problem in which we are interested. We cannot say whether a more general model should be preferred to a partial one without referring to a particular situation. For many problems, a partial model will be more useful. It will be easier to use, and any loss of accuracy may be very small indeed, offset by the advantages of simplicity.

Ceteris Paribus

This is a Latin phrase meaning "other things being equal." It is a key concept for any model-builder. Simplification is essentially a process invoking "ceteris paribus"; it implies that the things omitted from consideration—the "other things"—are not thought to be important for present purposes.

Static/Dynamic

The difference between static and dynamic models is related to the question of "ceteris paribus." A dynamic model is usually defined as a model that contains *within* itself a possibility for change over time. Change in a static model occurs as a result of change *outside* the model. Thus we can see that the more general a model is, the more likely it is to be dynamic, simply because fewer variables are left outside it. It is not a perfect one-to-one relationship, however. It is possible to have a completely general model that is also totally static.

The Marxist theory of history argues that each type of social organization contains conflicts that will eventually destroy it. It is, therefore, a dynamic model because change occurs as a result of the *necessary* conflict in the present. In comparison, a Keynesian model that relates the level of national income to various current factors is a static model. National income can only change if one of these factors changes. The model itself gives no reason why they should vary; thus, the change can only be a result of external factors.

A static model can compare only two situations: the situation before an external change and the one after the change has had its effect. It can only compare two equilibrium situations; it cannot show the path of adjustment from one equilibrium to another.

Dynamic models can give us this information. Consider two examples: one from microeconomics (the cobweb) and one from macroeconomics (the Harrod-Domar growth model).

The cobweb model was designed to predict the path of prices and the output of certain agricultural products when the market is not in equilibrium. The model is dynamic, because after the original movement from equilibrium (which originates outside the model, perhaps because of an unexpected crop failure), all changes are predicted by the model itself. This dynamic model predicts quite well for the markets for which it was designed, but its applicability is limited.

The Harrod-Domar model is a simple model of economic growth. Again, once the process is started, changes in national income will take place "ad infinitum." Increases in national income will lead to additions to the capital stock (investment). Increased investment will increase aggregate demand and thus lead to further increases in national income.

There are several points to be noted about this model. First, it is a genuinely dynamic model. The form of the model insures that changes in national income will continue.

Second, the model is highly unstable. It predicts that if the supply of total output is not equal to the demand for total

Two Dynamic Models

According to the cobweb theory, current output depends on the previous year's prices, while current prices depend on current output. Thus, high prices in one year will result in increased output and lower prices in the following year.

If production in the first year is Q_1, buyers will be willing to pay a price of P_1. At this price, producers will increase the next year's production to Q_2, for which output buyers will only be willing to pay P_2. This price will cause producers to reduce the next year's output to Q_3.

The Harrod-Domar model is a model of economic growth based on Keynes' ideas about the demand for total output. In this growth model, the supply of output depends on the capital stock, while the demand for output depends on additions to this capital stock (investment). The demand for total output is equal to the supply of total output only by sheer luck. There is nothing in the model to suggest that the economy will adjust to excess demand or excess supply.

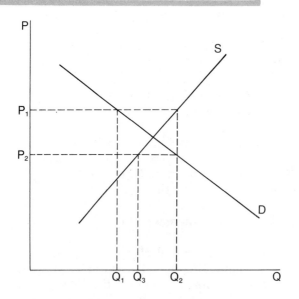

Figure A.

output, the economy will plunge into either depression or inflation. There is nothing in the model to bring the economy back into equilibrium. Since both depression and unemployment are thought to be undesirable, the Harrod-Domar growth model now acquires normative overtones. The equilibrium growth rate (called the warranted rate of growth) becomes the rate that policy wishes to achieve. Many models planning economic development use the Harrod-Domar model in this way.[8]

Since we live in a changing world, some people claim that static models are useless. This is not true. There are some economic questions for which a static model is satisfactory. For example, if we are interested in the extra revenue that the government could receive from an increased tax on cigarettes, we have to know how the sales of cigarettes will change as a result of the increase in price. Because we are only interested in a comparison of two equilibrium situations, a static model will be quite adequate for this purpose. For other purposes, a dynamic model may be required. Again, we can see that we cannot categorize one type of model as good and another as bad. It all depends on the job we want it to do.

Equilibrium/Disequilibrium

We have already met the terms "equilibrium" and "disequilibrium" in the discussion of dynamic and static models. It is time to define these terms more carefully, because some confusion does arise from the different usages of them.

A market or an economy is sometimes said to be in equilibrium if the market or markets concerned are "cleared." That is, equilibrium is said to exist if all goods that are offered for sale are also bought. This may sound like a reasonable definition, but, on further examination, it becomes clear that it is not useful to define equilibrium in this way.

There are several situations in which we should not say that equilibrium exists even though the market is cleared. First, buyers may have wanted to buy more than was available. Thus, even though the market was cleared, some consumers were disappointed. Second, sellers may have obtained lower prices than they had expected. They may have been willing to sell at a lower price rather than not

---

[8]See R. F. Miksell, *Economics of Foreign Aid* (Chicago: Aldine Publishing Co., 1968), for a discussion of this use of the Harrod-Domar model.

to sell their goods at all. This does not mean, however, that they will not reduce the amount they have available for sale on the next occasion. This situation is likely to occur in markets for perishable goods. Third, there may be markets that are always cleared. Saving is always equal to investment because what is saved must be invested.[9] The clearing of this market does not mean, however, that the amount of investment undertaken is the total amount that investors would have liked to have made.

These examples lead us to another, more useful definition of equilibrium. We can say that equilibrium exists if expectations are being realized and no plans are being frustrated. With this definition, markets in equilibrium will have been cleared, but not all situations in which markets have been cleared will be in equilibrium. Therefore, you can see that the cobweb is a disequilibrium dynamic model, because it predicts the behavior of the market when the plans of buyers and sellers have been frustrated. The Harrod-Domar model is an equilibrium dynamic model because it predicts the growth pattern that the economy will follow if planned saving equals planned investment. All static models are equilibrium models because they deal with comparisons of two equilibrium situations.

We see again how fruitless it is to categorize one particular type of model as good or bad. For some purposes, a disequilibrium model may be useful, while for others, an equilibrium model may be quite adequate.

Micro/Macro

The basic difference between micro- and macroeconomic models can be seen by looking at the derivation of these words. Both are from Greek; "micro" meaning small and "macro" meaning large. Microeconomics is usually concerned with the behavior of individual markets, while macroeconomics is concerned with the behavior of the whole economy. Economists have experienced difficulty in integrating these two branches of economics, mainly because they

---

[9]This identity between saving and investment refers to the disposition of physical output, not to money income. Everything that is produced must go somewhere. If it is not consumed, exported, or acquired by the government (i.e., if it is saved), it is invested. Some of this investment may not have been desired, however. For example, producers may be investing by making unplanned additions to their inventories.

have developed along very separate lines. Some attempts have been made to apply microeconomic concepts to macroeconomic problems, but success has been very limited — probably because the categories used in each branch are very different.

It should again be stressed that both branches of economics are important. It is useful to know both how the supply of rented accommodations would react to rent control (microeconomics) and how unemployment would change as a result of change in income tax rates (macroeconomics).

REASONS FOR BUILDING MODELS

Although we shall argue that the only viable final outcome from the economist's point of view is a predictive model, we shall see that description and understanding are vital stages in the process of arriving at acceptable predictive models. Explanation may be the desired final product, but a complete final explanation (in the popular sense of the word) is unattainable.

Explanation, understanding, and description are used here in their common, everyday meanings. Prediction, though, needs to be defined more precisely. A prediction is a statement about the type of behavior that we would expect if certain specified conditions existed. In other words, a prediction is a testable proposition derived from a model. It is *not* necessarily a statement about future events; it is simply a contingent proposition. Much confusion results from an imperfect understanding of the meaning of prediction in scientific inquiry. It is not a prophecy. It is the answer to the question, "What would happen if...?" For example, the statement, "Since gold was the monetary standard of the time, one would expect inflation to result from the large gold imports into Europe during the sixteenth century," is a prediction that follows from the more general proposition, "An increase in the supply of money will be accompanied by inflation." The fact that we are talking about events four hundred years ago does not make it less of a prediction. In fact, economists are often interested in the prediction of past events to test the usefulness of their models in analyzing today's world.

On the other hand, our everyday definition of explanation differs from that used by many philosophers of social science, who define explanation simply as the prediction of past events. While we could use the term in this latter sense, it is not very useful to do so; it reduces prediction to forecasting—that is, the prediction of future events. Yet explanation as it is commonly understood still remains a problem. To explain usually means "to offer reasons for or a cause of."[10] That is, to ask for an explanation is to ask for knowledge of *why* things happen. Scientists would like to be able to answer these questions, but there are many problems attached to testing the validity of the answers.[11] So we have to be satisfied with prediction—that is, answering the question, "What would happen if . . . ?" Prediction is, of course, a very important activity in its own right. For example, it is important to know what will happen if minimum wage legislation is introduced, or what will happen if the supply of money is increased—even if we can never be completely sure why the results occur.

It is sometimes claimed that the principal goal of model-building is to increase our understanding. This statement is usually made in a very loose way and is often made in defense of a particular model or set of models. Such models may not in themselves yield useful predictions, but when refined, they may become extremely useful. The best example in recent times is the *General Theory*. Keynes attempted to overthrow the existing orthodoxy, which he believed had persisted in asking the wrong questions. Yet if the student reviews the early Keynesian literature, he or she will find numerous examples of the model being corrected, amended, or reinterpreted in an attempt to make Keynes' statement clearer and more satisfactory. Keynes himself did not derive any clear-cut predictions of the relationship between national income and the rate of interest. It was left to later writers to develop precise predictions of this type, but their work depended on the understanding provided by Keynes.[12]

A model that increases our understanding but does not yield predictions is only a prototype. Such a model is well known to the research worker, who may go through many such prototypes. Because economic researchers are not always willing to provide information on the various steps

---

[10]William Morris (ed.), *The American Heritage Dictionary of the English Language.* (Boston: American Heritage Publishing Co. and Houghton Mifflin Co., 1973.)

[11]See Chapter 6.

[12]See, for example, A. Hansen, *A Guide to Keynes.* (New York: McGraw-Hill Book Co., 1953.)

they must go through, they sometimes give students the idea that arriving at an appropriate model is relatively easy. Eventually, it is necessary to derive a model that yields useful predictions. We are concerned not only with understanding the economic system but also with being able to manipulate it to improve it. Manipulation, however, necessitates prediction. Similar remarks can be made about descriptive economic models. They may be final products from the point of view of individual researchers, but they cannot be considered in this light by economics as a whole.

This should not be interpreted to mean that description and understanding play no part in model-building. They are vital if we are to build adequate predictive models. When the results of research appear, they are often presented as a reliable predictive model. The reader of these results has not seen the process that has resulted in such a model. Generally, the researcher's path has been one of the building and modification of unsatisfactory models.[13] It is at this stage that understanding has been increased (by a bad model) and fed back into the research in the form of an improved model. The role of description is even more basic. No models can be build without classification, and the descriptive process is an important way in which categories are formed and later modified to fit the situation in which we are interested.

---

[13]See Chapter 6.

QUESTIONS

1. What is the basic distinction between positive and normative statements? Why is it necessary for the model-builder to distinguish between them?

2. Some economists working in the field of economic development claim that positive economic theory is not a satisfactory tool for working on the problems of developing countries. They claim that a more committed approach is needed. Do you agree?

3. Which group of people is likely to believe that a high rate of unemployment is preferable to a high rate of inflation? Why do you think they hold this particular value judgment?

4. Why is knowing the purpose of the model more important than knowing the category of the model for example, whether it is static or dynamic? Why would it be wrong to make an unqualified statement such as "The model is useless because it is static?"

5. What are the justifications for model-building that some economists would give? How would you criticize these reasons? Which is the most acceptable to you?

PROBLEMS OF MODEL-BUILDING

5

"The use of models distorts the truth."

"Models do not tell the whole truth."

"All men are different."

"People are not always rational."

"Man is not just an economic animal; he has emotions that make him interested in more than his own well-being."

Criticisms such as these are often leveled at economic models. (Some, of course, also apply to models in other sciences.) The principal criticisms fall into two categories. First, there are general criticisms of the process of model-building itself. Second, there are specific criticisms of certain assumptions used in particular models. Criticisms of the first type apply to model-building in all sciences; if we accept their validity for economics, then we must accept their validity for other sciences. The second set of criticisms is specific to economic models, and it is often based on a mistaken understanding of the purposes of particular models.

DISTORTION, OR "THE USE OF MODELS DISTORTS THE TRUTH"

The problem of distortion was introduced in Chapter 2. Since all models omit some factors in the real world, and since the classification of factors in the model itself is a result of subjective evaluation, models are necessarily distorted reflections of the real world. One cannot disagree with this broad point as it stands, but it is necessary to evaluate the effects of distortion.

We have already seen that omission can be essential and useful; only rarely can it be harmful. Types of omission in description seemed to fall into six groups. These were:

A. Voluntary
  1. Simplification
  2. Lack of interest
  3. Information assumed to be available elsewhere in a more convenient form
  4. Misleading the audience

B. Involuntary
  1. Limitations of the medium
  2. Limitations in perception

These same groups can apply to omission in economic models, whatever their purpose.

Some factors are omitted from economic models because of lack of interest: that is, they are omitted because they are thought to be of no importance to the question at hand. For example, the state of the weather is omitted from most models of consumer demand because it is not thought to be important. This omission may, of course, be a mistake for some goods (e.g., umbrellas). Such an omission would then be a result of limited perception and would be involuntary.

Other factors are omitted voluntarily from economic models because information about them is assumed to be available elsewhere. Economic models usually accept consumer preferences as given, leaving the explanation of these preferences to psychologists.

Economic models also omit details because of the limitations of the medium. For instance, many models of international trade are expressed graphically; because of this two-dimensional representation, they tend to deal only with the trade of two goods between two countries that have only two factors of production.

There are also economic models in which omissions are intentional in order to mislead other users. A model-builder who wishes to show that a certain industry should be free of government intervention is likely to build a model that does not consider the pollution caused by that industry.

The first type of omission — simplification — is very important in economic models. Because economic phenomena are so complex, it would be impossible and useless to include all possible factors. The inclusion of more variables, or the disaggregation of a single variable into several different ones (for example, by breaking down "Labor" into several different types of labor), may increase the accuracy of the model, but only at the cost of increasing its complexity. In all model-building, a point is reached at which the increase in accuracy is just not worth the increase in complexity. This point depends both on the benefits of the increased accuracy and on the cost of the increased complexity (for example, the cost and the availability of computer facilities).

The process of increasing the accuracy of the model by increasing the number of variables needs to be discussed further. Increasing the number of variables may increase either the *descriptive* accuracy of the model or its *predictive* accuracy. Increasing one type of accuracy does not automatically also increase the other. This point is connected to the argument that is made frequently in this book: that one cannot interpret a good predictive model as being necessarily descriptively accurate.

Little can be added to the list of effects of omission discussed in Chapter 2. It is useful, however, to re-emphasize the extent to which omissions can be harmful in model building. Generally, they are only harmful when we are not aware of them. If we are aware of the factors that are being omitted and, at the same time, understand the reason for their omission, we are not likely to be misled into thinking that the model is a mirror image of reality. We shall be aware of the relationship that it has with the real world. Consequently, if the model performs inadequately, we shall have some idea of the factors that might be added to it to obtain a better model.

These points are also relevant to the distortion caused by classification. Since people each have their own idiosyncrasies, the classification of these individuals into groups will inevitably result in some distortion. Yet some classification is essential for simplification. Therefore, to avoid the problems arising from this type of distortion, it is necessary to be aware of the status of the classification. One should be aware that the grouping is simply a convenient simplification; it is not and should not be implied that all the contents are identical. It is only true that, in each particular model, the elements resemble each other more than they resemble non-members of the group. If this is not true, the classification is inappropriate for that model and should be replaced.

UNIVERSAL MODELS, OR "MODELS DO NOT TELL THE WHOLE TRUTH"

"Demand obviously depends upon fashion, advertising, personal taste, and so forth. Economic models cannot explain these factors and are, therefore, bad models." This criticism and others like it are frequently leveled against economic models. The inference is that, because economic models cannot explain or predict some phenomena, they cannot explain or predict any phenomena at all. When put this way, the criticism does not seem very cogent but, nevertheless, it does appear with some frequency.

Like many other criticisms of economic models, this arises from a misunderstanding of the use of models. Models are built to answer particular types of questions, and their performance should be judged in relation to them. Because they are necessarily simplifications of reality, it is both unfair and unwise to expect models to answer questions for which they were not designed.

Most economic models are designed to answer questions such as, "What would be the effect on government revenues of an increased tax on cigarettes?" or, "What would be the effect of increased grain prices on the price of meat in domestic shops?" The validity of economic models should be judged on the accuracy with which they answer such questions. Good models are usually capable of answering different questions of the same type. A model built to answer the question about meat prices could probably be used to answer a question about the effect of changing fish prices. Some more variables could be added to the model to show the relationship between the demand for meat and the price of a substitute for meat, such as fish. However many variables are added, it would still not be appropriate to use this model to answer a question such as, "Would an advertising campaign using the slogan *Meat makes you strong* have any effect on the demand for meat?" This question is concerned with the way tastes are changed, and economic models are not intended and are not suitable to answer such questions. Only if they are told that such a campaign *would* increase peoples' preferences for meat can economists say anything about the effects of this campaign on prices and quantities.

Similarly, the model built by social psychologists to answer the question of the effect of the campaign on tastes cannot be extended to answer the questions asked by economists. They are different types of questions, and different types of models are necessary to answer them. There is no model that could answer all questions. Such a construct would simply be a duplication of the real world, and we saw in Chapter 2 the problems that would accompany this.

MODELS AND THE "FACTS"

The models that are built by economists are limited by the availability of data. This limitation operates in two ways.

First, the concepts used in the theoretical formulation may not be directly observable. For example, studies of the rate of return to higher education have to include an estimate of the costs of higher education. These costs include not only the direct costs of tuition, books, and so on, but also the opportunity costs of foregone earnings—the money that students would have earned had they not attended college. These opportunity costs could not be observed directly, since no money actually changed hands. They can only be estimated indirectly by noting the salaries earned by high school graduates who did not attend college.

Second, necessary data may not be available. In such cases, it would be possible to collect the data that have not yet been collected. The collection of national income statistics is a relatively recent activity; it is in part a result of the demands made by the use of various Keynesian models for the control of national economies. Although the construction of models may induce the collection of useful data, the testing and the use of such models must be delayed until this occurs. Most data are collected on the basis of an implicit model and thus may not be suitable for testing another model. Data collected on the basis of the Keynesian model, using Keynesian classifications, may not be suitable for testing a macroeconomic model that uses different categories.

THE UNIQUENESS OF THE INDIVIDUAL, OR "ALL MEN ARE DIFFERENT"

This, perhaps, is the criticism used most against models in the social sciences. A simple version of the argument would be something like the following: "Social sciences are concerned with the behavior of people. Each person is an individual with his own idiosyncratic behavior patterns. 'People' is not a homogeneous entity like those examined by the physical sciences. They are not like 'iron' or 'oxygen.' Therefore, it is inappropriate to make models of their behavior." This version of the criticism is extremely naive and contains two basic fallacies.

First, the conclusion does not follow logically from the first part of the statement. The fact that each person has his or her own idiosyncratic behavior pattern does not preclude the building of models. Each person may behave perfectly consistently, even though he might behave differently from others. If his behavior is consistent, it is possible to build models of it.

Indeed, we do this every day in a very informal way. We have some expectations of how a particular person will behave in certain situations. The better we know this person, the more precise and reliable these expectations will be, though to predict an individual's reaction in one situation, it is not necessary to know his reactions in other, dissimilar situations. In other words, we have certain implicit models of an individual's behavior that yield predictions about his or her behavior in given situations. The more sophisticated the model, the more precise the predictions, and the less likely they are to be refuted.

Second, the criticism is confused on two points. The first point is concerned with the statement that 'people' is not a homogeneous entity. This has emotive connotations, and it is important to examine its meaning in this particular context. There would be little disagreement with the interpretation that describes people as being diverse in their tastes, their aspirations, and their fears. This variety gives some of the spice to life. To be of any use for our purposes, however, this interpretation must be reformulated. To have an operational meaning, this statement might be interpreted to mean that the behavior of individuals is so idiosyncratic that one can observe no regularities in the behavior of large groups of people. This is an empirical statement that can be confirmed or rejected by examining the behavior of large groups. To some extent, this statement can be seen to be false, for one *can* observe some regularities in behavior. Rural families tend to have more children than do urban families; rural areas in the United States are likely to vote Republican, and urban areas are more likely to vote Democratic; in higher education, boys tend to study math and physics, while girls tend to study English.

The second point of confusion is related to this: The uniqueness of the individual is often interpreted to mean that one or more people will always act in a way other than that predicted by the model. There would be little disagreement with this statement; it does not invalidate the use of models, however. Very few, if any, models are of the form, "Under given circumstances, all people will always behave in such-and-such a way." Models are usually of the form, "Under given circumstances, there is a certain probability that people will behave in such and such a way."[1] That is, most models in the social sciences are probabilistic (that is, based upon probabilities). Thus, it is irrevelant that some people in the group being studied will sometimes behave differently. So long as the group as a whole tends to behave in a regular manner, we can build models of its behavior.

It is sometimes thought that the probabilistic nature of models used in the social sciences makes them qualitatively inferior to models used in the physical sciences. For example, consider two fairly well-known models used in the physical sciences.

The first example deals with the study of projectiles. Suppose we were concerned with dropping parcels of food on a specific target.[2] A simple model to predict where a parcel will hit the ground would say that x (the distance in feet between the point at which the parcel was released and the point where it hits the ground) depends upon the speed of the plane, the height of the plane above the ground, and the force of gravity. This model predicts very precisely the point at which the parcel will hit the ground.[3] It seems to be very far removed from the probabilistic models used by the social sciences. Nevertheless, this model does not predict very accurately except in a laboratory situation, because it ignores factors such as air resistance, topography of the ground, deviations of the flight path of the plane from a perfectly hor-

---

[1] See Chapter 8.
[2] The parcels are very well wrapped, and parachutes are not used.
[3] The equation is:

$$x = v \sqrt{\frac{2h}{g}}$$

where v is the forward speed of the plane in feet per second, h is the height of the plane in feet above the ground, and g is the acceleration due to the force of gravity and is a constant equal to 32 feet per second per second.

izontal course, and so forth. These are the factors that are placed under "ceteris paribus" in laboratory experiments. Their inclusion in the model of the falling food parcel would improve the accuracy of its predictions.[4]

So what does this really mean? By including more variables in the model, we are increasing the probability of obtaining accurate predictions from it. There is then no qualitative difference between this kind of model and the kind of model that we are accustomed to using in the social sciences. Both types of models are essentially of a probabilistic nature, and the probability of obtaining correct predictions is likely to increase as the number of variables placed in the category of "ceteris paribus" decreases. The difference between the two types of models is quantitative. For the most part, the number of variables that must be considered in the case of a physical phenomenon is likely to be smaller than in the case of a social one. Therefore, for any two models containing the same number of variables (starting, of course, with the most important), the physical model is likely to yield predictions with a higher degree of accuracy than the social science model. This does not necessarily reflect an inferior quality of social science models, although this is always a strong possibility. It may simply reflect the relative complexity of social phenomena.

The second example comes from the field of genetics. The model of heredity proposed by Gregor Mendel is illustrated in Figure 5.1. It refers to the shape of peas. R is the gene that produces round, smooth peas, while r is the gene that produces wrinkled peas. R is the dominant gene; any pea that contains R will produce round, smooth peas. In his experiments, however, Mendel observed that plants that produced round, smooth peas could also produce offspring that had wrinkled peas. His model was built to explain this phenomenon. He assumed that each plant contained two of the genes determining the shape of the pea, so that each plant in the first generation had the genes RR or rr. In the

---

[4]In many cases, the increased accuracy will not compensate for the increased costs of using a model with more variables. The crew of a plane has too many other things to worry about without being burdened with a twelve variable model when the two variable model will do almost as well. The same model can be applied to aerial bombing; again the crew of a bomber would probably find it worthwhile to use only the simple model. Modern ballistic missiles probably require the use of the more complex model, however.

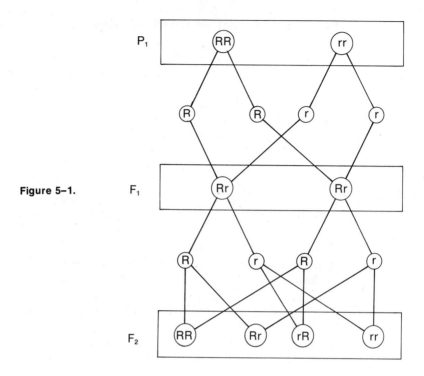

Figure 5–1.

next generation, only one gene from each plant combined with one gene from another to form a new plant.

Thus, in the first generation, P_1, we have the pure plants, *RR* and *rr*, which produce only smooth or only wrinkled peas, respectively. These plants are now crossbred to produce generation F_1. Both plants in F_1 are *Rr* and, because *R* is dominant, produce round, smooth peas. The plants of the F_1 generation are then allowed to cross-pollinate to produce the next generation, F_2. It is possible for the plants in F_2 to be *RR, Rr, Rr,* or *rr*; that is, three plants with round, smooth peas may be produced to each plant with wrinkled peas. If the genes combine at random (if there is no tendency for *R* to combine with *R* rather than with *r*, and vice versa, we can predict that, in a large number of F_2 generation plants, three plants with smooth peas will have been created to every one with wrinkled peas. Although we cannot predict the characteristics of any one particular plant, we can predict the characteristics of the group as a whole. This is exactly what we do in many models in social science.

"PEOPLE ARE NOT ALWAYS RATIONAL"

A criticism closely related to the concept of the uniqueness of the individual is often directed against economic models; that is, they assume rational "economic man." Since it seems that individuals do not always behave rationally, economic models are seen as invalid.

This argument is confused. First, consider the concept of rationality. In common speech, rationality often implies a moral judgment about a person's objectives; to the economist, it usually means the pursuit of given ends by appropriate means. Thus, it might be reasonable in everyday conversation to show that people are not rational by describing their ends as trivial, misguided, and so forth, but this does not show that they are irrational in the economic sense. People are economically irrational only if they are not using the most efficient means open to them to achieve given ends.

Second, this criticism misunderstands the role of the assumption of rationality in economic models. This assumption does not imply that each person consciously evaluates every action to see whether it is the most appropriate for his purpose; it simply means that his behavior will tend to follow a pattern that would have been predicted if he had planned his actions beforehand. Thus, we cannot say that a certain type of behavior shows that an individual *is* behaving rationally; it simply shows that he is acting *as if* he were rational.

"MAN IS NOT JUST AN ECONOMIC BEING"

Economic man is a central concept of economic theory and is therefore the focus of much of the criticism of economic models. It is assumed that he makes choices that will maximize his own utility.[5] The criticisms of the concept of economic man may be either indirect, aimed at the concepts of rationality and choice, or direct.

It seems impossible that economic man does now or ever did exist. The concept gives rise to a picture of a population of inhuman calculating machines that evaluate each possible course of action before deciding on the one that will further their own selfish ends. This interpretation results from a misunderstanding of the use of the concept in economic theory.

---

[5]In terms of economic theory, utility means happiness or satisfaction, not usefulness.

First, economic man is not necessarily entirely selfish. His own utility may (and probably does) depend on the utility of others. There is no reason why the concept of economic man should preclude the economic analysis of charity.

Second, economic theory is not concerned with *how* an individual reaches a decision. Thus, it is not important from the point of view of economic models for individuals to calculate the effects of all possible alternatives; that is, it is not important that individuals should *in fact* be perfect economic men. It is only important that this concept should yield useful predictions about economic *behavior*. Many useful predictions have been derived in this way.

The concept of rationality is closely related to that of economic man, and the discussion of the latter also applies to rationality. There are other aspects of the concept of rationality that need to be considered more carefully, however.

We have already defined economic rationality as the choosing of appropriate means to achieve given ends. It is important to understand that it is possible to act rationally in the economic sense and still be mistaken. For example, it is possible to choose means that are appropriate *given existing information*, but that would not be appropriate if better information were available. Thus, false information can result in mistaken choices, but it need not result in irrational ones. Rationality refers only to the means (and, therefore, the information) available to the individual at a given time.

It should also be emphasized that rationality within the context of economic models should be interpreted neither normatively nor descriptively. Rationality is not a prescription for the way people should behave. It is merely an *assumption* about their behavior that enables us to derive useful predictions. Similarly, it is not a description to help us classify "men" and "non-men." There has been a tendency in some behavioral sciences to define the features that distinguish men from beasts, and rationality has featured prominently in such lists. It must be understood that the concept does not and should not serve this function in economics. In economic models, economic men are assumed to be rational, but the *definition* of men is decided on other criteria.

Rational behavior for the individual may be different from that for the group as a whole; much economic policy is centered on changing the incentives for individuals so that behavior that is rational for the individual will also be beneficial for the group. For example, in times of inflation, consumers will expect price increases to continue in the future.

They will therefore have an incentive to buy certain goods such as consumer durables now rather than in the future, when the price will be higher. This increase in consumer demand will increase prices still further. Thus, by acting rationally as individuals, the consumers will have caused the very increase in prices that they feared. The policy problem then becomes one of changing the expectation of future price increases.

The concept of choice — that is, the existence of alternatives — is also obviously related both to rationality and to economic man. If choice does not exist, then economic models that assume its existence will be redundant.

The most common criticism of this concept is that the poor cannot choose. While appealing as a political slogan, this criticism is not convincing when applied to economic models. The possibility of choice in economic models does not imply that anyone can have anything he chooses. Indeed, this would negate the study of economics, which is essentially the study of the allocation of scarce resources among competing ends. Economic models explicitly place constraints on choice, and the interesting problems are usually those concerned with how much of one good one has to give up to obtain some other good. Thus, choice exists for the poor as well as for the rich. There are simply greater constraints on the choices of the poor than there are on those of the rich. Most of the discussions about poverty programs are based on their relative abilities to ease these constraints.

SUMMARY

The first three objections to model-building are objections to the use of models in general, even though they may have been formulated as criticisms of specific economic models. All models in any science distort the truth, give less than the whole picture, and need appropriate data to be tested. Although these are real problems, they are not insurmountable. Indeed, the first two problems can also be seen as strengths. They are the result of simplification, which is a necessary and useful process. The other objections to economic models refer to the assumptions of specific models;

they contain misunderstandings of the way the assumptions are used and of the proper interpretation of the model.

QUESTIONS

1. An event has just taken place that leads an observer to remark, "Oh, isn't that just like John to behave like that!" What would the speaker have to know about John before he could make such a statement? What information about John would be irrelevant?

2. Discuss the statement: "Because the social sciences deal with people, and because each individual is unique, then predictions about their behavior are likely to be mistaken."

3. What is meant by probabilistic models? Would it be correct to argue that only social science models are probabilistic?

4. "Economic man is an unacceptable assumption because it distorts human nature and precludes the possibility of genuine human love, charity, and so on." Discuss.

5. From the following list of figures, what generalizations can you draw about the behavior of the people concerned?

Age (years)	Sex	Math Test Score
15.0	F	90
14.6	M	88
14.8	M	89
15.2	F	76
14.5	F	72
14.9	F	60
15.3	M	93
15.4	F	89
15.1	M	82
15.5	M	85

TESTING MODELS AND THEORIES

6

Facts were never pleasing to him. He acquired them with reluctance and got rid of them with relief.

—J. M. Barrie

POSITIVE AND NORMATIVE AGAIN

What is a good model?

There are two issues involved in the answer to this question. One has to choose both the criteria to judge the performance of the model, and the degree of accuracy or inaccuracy that is acceptable. The question of criteria is a positive one, and its answer is related to the purpose for which the model is intended. The degree of accuracy is a normative judgment that depends on the values and the requirements of the model user.

Because of their very nature as abstractions and simplifications, no models can claim complete accuracy, although many in the physical sciences can claim very high levels of accuracy. Since models are never completely accurate, it is necessary to make a decision about the amount of inaccuracy that we will find acceptable. How accurate must a model be before we are prepared to use it?

There are two kinds of inaccuracy that occur in model-building. One is a result of omitting relevant variables, while the other is a result of including irrelevant variables, thus obtaining invalid results. Both of these problems are discussed in an introductory manner in Chapter 8. For the purposes of this chapter, however, it is sufficient to note that they exist. They both pose the same question, "How much of each type of inaccuracy is acceptable?"

Strictly speaking, this question cannot be answered by the economist acting as an economist. It is a normative question for the model user and can only be answered with respect to his own subjective evaluation of the usefulness of the model. There are statistical conventions that can help him in this evaluation; these are discussed in Chapter 8. Ultimately the model user must make his own decision about the amount of inaccuracy that he can accept — and this is a normative judgment.

SOME DEFINITIONS

Before discussing the positive aspects of testing models, it is desirable for us to define some terms. Some of these terms will already be familiar from earlier parts of this book, but they have not yet been defined. They all appear quite frequently in discussions of economic models, although they are not always used with the same meaning by other authors. Here they are given precise and, we believe, useful meanings to facilitate our discussion of testing models.

Postulate. A fundamental assertion that is believed to be true but that is unproved and probably unprovable.

Assumption. An assertion that is not necessarily believed to be true, but is believed to be useful for present purposes because it simplifies the problem.

Proposition. A deduction that follows logically from the postulates and the assumptions and is the basis of prediction.

Prediction. A statement concerning events in the real world under given conditions.

Forecast. A statement concerning events in the real world at a given time.

Some of these terms seem very similar. The reasons for differentiating them will soon (we hope) become clear.

Postulates and assumptions seem the most similar. An example may help to clarify the difference. Suppose we are constructing a model of the fish market. When we consider the actions of the buyers of fish, we postulate that each buyer has preferences for many different commodities, including fish, and that he can rank them in order of preference. We also postulate that he will choose to buy those goods that give him the most satisfaction at his present income and at current prices. This postulate may seem reasonable to us as a result of our experience of the world. We may reason that we make our choices in this way and, therefore, most other people will also do so. Yet however reasonable these postulates may seem, they can never be proved. We have no way of measuring the satisfaction that different people obtain from different goods. We can ask people whether they make choices in this way, but this cannot prove or disprove the postulates—even if we can be sure that they are telling the truth. By asking these questions, we are not directly testing the postulates. We are only testing whether people know that they act in this way.

Some writers have decided that it is unnecessary to test postulates, since they are so obvious and so much a part of everyday experience. This view implies, however, that there is an absolute, objective reality that can be discovered by experience. It implies that we are not deceived by limited perception and can thus observe our experiences objectively. This position would be difficult to maintain. Our observation—our common everyday experience—tells us that the sun moves while the earth stands still. If we had no way to test this experience, we would still hold this belief. Everyday experience is not a reliable guide to the truth. Postulates, therefore, must remain unprovable.

By comparison, we may make the assumption that there are very many small buyers; this is the assumption of perfect competition. There may, however, be one very large buyer and several smaller buyers; one large firm may buy a large proportion of the fish in the wholesale market. Yet if the assumption of perfect competition gives a model that answers our original questions satisfactorily, then we are justified in simplifying our model by making this assumption. It does not mean that we think that there really is perfect competition; it just means that we find this assumption convenient.

Postulates are often given the status of definitions or axioms. Used in this way, maximization of utility is no longer an aspect of consumer behavior that the model-builder believes to be true. It becomes instead a defining characteristic of consumer behavior and runs the risk of giving rise to untestable statements purported to be scientific "proofs." It is very easy for a person to find himself "proving" that a certain behavior enables a consumer to maximize utility simply because the consumer would not have behaved in that way if it had *not* enabled him to maximize utility. This is a definitional use of postulates that has not proved very useful in economics because it cannot produce testable hypotheses. In general, scientists do not find it useful to treat postulates as definitions, although studies such as logic or Euclidean geometry do find it useful.

As we have seen, prediction causes some confusion. A prediction is a statement about the events that would occur in the real world under certain conditions. It may refer to either future or past events. The only difference between predictions of past and future events is that the former can be tested immediately, whereas the latter can only be tested sometime in the future.

There is a conceptual difference between predictions of future events and forecasting. Forecasting is simply the practice of making a statement about what will happen at a particular time in the future. A statement about the GNP in 1984 or the rate of investment in 1980 is a forecast. A prediction is a statement about what will happen in a particular situation, such as, "If the city of Chicago increases its property tax, rents will rise by less than the amount of the tax." Predictions are sometimes called "contingent propositions"; that is, they are propositions about events in the real world that are contingent (conditional) on the occurrence of other events. In general, scientists are interested in prediction, while policy makers are interested in forecasting.

In practice, this distinction is blurred, because forecasts are usually themselves contingent propositions. Statements about the value of the GNP in 1984 are forecasts made on the basis of current or expected government policy. If such expectations are not realized, the forecast will be invalid. Indeed, there are usually many forecasts about the same variable, each of which depends on different conditions occurring between the present and the relevant future time period.

The conceptual difference between prediction and forecasting should not be forgotten, however. Confusion between these two activities lends weight to criticisms of the scientific status of economics. One often hears claims that economic *theory* cannot predict accurately, which is then "proved" by references to numerous erroneous forecasts. If one is aware of the difference between forecasting and prediction, it becomes obvious that a failure in *forecasting* does not necessarily entail a failure in *prediction*. Erroneous forecasts may occur simply because factors occur that were not expected. Thus, the forecast will have been proved wrong, but the prediction cannot have been proved right or wrong, since the prediction was contingent on the non-occurrence of these unexpected factors.

POSITIVE CRITERIA FOR SATISFACTORY MODELS

It is now time to return to the question with which this chapter started. What is a good model?

The first reaction to this question is often closely related to the following statement: The more closely a model is related to its subject, the more satisfactory it is. This is a condition called *isomorphism*. Classical isomorphism involves a one-to-one relationship between the model and its subject. That is, with classical isomorphism, all variables and the relationships between them that exist in the subject being studied also exist in the model. Because of the necessity for simplification, it seems impossible for any model to have this property. Therefore, the argument about the closeness of the relationship between model and subject takes classical isomorphism as the ideal—the most desirable model. This argument relates somewhat to the ideas in Chapter 2. It was shown then that the use of this concept results in the inclusion of more and more detail and eventually reduces the effectiveness of the description. A similar process occurs when this criterion is used to evaluate models. Models of social phenomena are then likely to become so complex as to be useless.

The criteria for judging the aptness of a description must be related to the purposes of that description. Descriptions are designed to answer certain questions; they are apt if they answer these questions adequately. Therefore, the fitness of the description depends on its function. This also applies to economic models. The criteria by which a particular model is judged *must* depend on its purpose. There is no one criterion, such as classical isomorphism, that can be used to evaluate the performance of all economic models.

Descriptive models can be judged by criteria that should be familiar from Chapter 2. Are the categories used appropriate to the question being asked? Is the medium appropriate? Are the categories clear and unambiguous? Is any overlap between categories avoided? Is the emphasis of the description relevant to the question it is designed to answer?

It is difficult to evaluate objectively models designed to increase our understanding. If it is accepted that a model may increase our understanding by giving rise to other more precise models, then one cannot judge the former model in isolation from the latter. We can only say that a model has been an efficient tool for increasing our understanding of the economic system after the other group of models has been built; that is, models that increase understanding can only be evaluated in retrospect.

We can think of four different ways in which an explanation may be judged. Let us take as an example a common explanation of the pattern of rainfall. It is observed that in the United Kingdom there is some relationship between the level of rainfall and the altitude of the land. Generally, high ground receives more rainfall than low ground. The common explanation is that air laden with moisture arrives from the West. As it reaches high ground, it is forced upward into colder air and, as it cools, the moisture condenses and falls as rain.

One possibility is to judge this explanatory model by testing the plausibility of its assumptions. Many simplifying assumptions are made. For example, it is assumed that the amount of clouds will be the same each year and that their distribution over the year will be the same. Can we accept that it is reasonable to make these assumptions? Obviously, the amount of clouds will not be exactly the same each year. The essence of model-building, however, is to simplify phenomena by placing similar occurrences in the same categories. How different does the amount of clouds have to be before the amounts are assumed to be different? What *is* a plausible assumption? This first seemingly reasonable criterion is already giving us trouble.

A second way in which an explanation may be judged is by examining its internal consistency. Are its assumptions consistent with each other? Do the deductions of the model follow logically from the assumptions? This is, of course, a criterion that all models should satisfy, but it is not a sufficient test of a model. The Ptolemaic model of the universe is internally consistent, but in the light of what we know now, we would not consider it a good explanation of the solar system. Moreover, this criterion gives us no way to distinguish between two different but internally consistent models. The common model of the distribution of rainfall is internally consistent, but so is an alternative that explains the pattern of rainfall by suggesting that a Rain God lives on the top of each hill and makes rain. It could be argued that the higher the hill, the more powerful the Rain God, and thus the more rain he makes.

Next, we can judge an explanation by its external consistency. This criterion is connected to judging it by testing the plausibility of its assumptions. Some assumptions are or could be deductions from other models. This is why we con-

The Ptolemaic Model of the Universe

This model of the universe was generally accepted during most of the Middle Ages. As with most ideas, many people were involved in its development, but the Greek astronomer Ptolemy is usually thought to be responsible for the statement of its most significant features. In this model, the earth was the center of the universe, and all the other planets of the solar system, including the sun, revolved around it. All other stars were fixed. Since they thought that the planets could not stay in the sky by their own volition, these early astronomers hypothesized that each planet was attached to a crystal sphere (crystal so that more distant planets could be seen through it) that would revolve and take the planet with it. Thus, the universe was seen as a huge sphere with the earth at its center and crystal spheres surrounding it like the skins of an onion. The fixed stars were attached to the last sphere.

By the fourteenth century, it was becoming clear that this model did not yield very good predictions of the positions of the planets. Attempts were made to modify the model by mounting each planet on a smaller sphere attached to the original large sphere. The movement of both spheres together produced movements that were more consistent with those actually observed. Successive modifications of this type eventually produced an extremely complicated model.

sider the Ptolemaic model of the universe and the Rain God model of rainfall unsatisfactory. We know of no reason why the planets should move on a set of crystal spheres, but we do know of a reason—the force of gravity—why they should move in ellipses around the sun. Similarly, we have no external proof of the existence of Rain Gods, but we do have proof of differences in temperature at various altitudes and of the ability of air to retain moisture at different temperatures. This creates other questions, however. How do we know that the deductions of other models are correct? For example, how do we know that the force of gravity acts as we say it does? How do we decide that it is necessary to introduce these deductions as assumptions in a later model? That is, how simple or complicated does our model have to be? This third method of testing an explanation is equivalent to testing the predictions of other models. Each statement in the explanation is a prediction of another model. We have more faith in an explanation if these other models have proved to be reliable in producing adequate predictions.

Finally, we can judge an explanation by its predictions. If it yields predictions that are correct for a satisfactory proportion of the cases we consider, then it is a good explanation. This not only avoids the problems raised by the first three criteria, but it also solves them. With this criterion, a good assumption is one that yields correct predictions.

On the other hand, there are other problems raised by the use of this criterion to judge explanatory models. The model could predict correctly and still be wrong. That is, the same predictions can be derived from many different explanatory models. For example, our explanation of the pattern of rainfall may yield the same predictions as an explanation in terms of greater or lesser Rain Gods living on the tops of hills. The accuracy of their predictions gives us no way of differentiating between these explanations.

Ultimately, the validity of an explanation depends on belief. We accept the explanation based on differences in temperature because it seems more plausible in the light of our set of values and experiences. There is no scientific way of testing it.[1] Naturally, the more reliable the predictions of an explanatory model tend to be, the more confidence we have in it *as an explanation*. This is a natural tendency, but it is not a legitimate scientific procedure.

As scientists, we are primarily interested in explanation. It is our tragedy that we are never able to test these explanations scientifically. We can only test predictive models and try to gain some enlightenment from them.

At first sight, it would appear that predictive accuracy is the only test we need to apply to predictive models. While this test is necessary, it is not always sufficient. There are other standards we should apply.

Suppose we have two models that yield the same predictions. How do we choose between them?

---

[1]Not even testing each stage of the explanation—e.g., moisture content at lower temperatures, temperature at different heights, and so forth—would "prove" the explanation. On the other hand, it could be argued that the Rain Gods make the temperature seem lower. If this seems ridiculous, think of the Freudian theory of the subconscious. The subconscious in this theory plays a role similar to that of the invisible Rain God—the prime cause but yet, by its very nature, unobservable.

We must apply two other tests.

1. Are the models externally consistent?

2. Is one model simpler than the other? If this is so, we should choose the simpler model, because it is less expensive to use. Note that we can make this decision only because we are simply interested in the accuracy of predictions.

It is important to stress, however, that on strictly positive grounds, we should not interpret the model as being descriptively accurate. If we obtain accurate predictions from a model of the fish market that assumes perfect competition, we cannot then say that the market is *in fact* perfectly competitive; we can only say that it behaves *as if* it were perfectly competitive. So we cannot test the *reality* of assumptions by the accuracy of the resultant predictions; we can only test the *usefulness* of assumptions. In this case, perfect competition is a useful *simplification* by which we reduce the actions of many buyers and sellers of different sizes to an orderly pattern that we call perfect competition. This is not a *description* of the market structure, since we have defined the market only by its behavior and not by its own characteristics. If we define perfect competition as a market with many small buyers and sellers — and "small" is given a definite meaning — then the concept of perfect competition can be used as a description of the actual market. It is a description of the market in terms of its most important characteristics. In short, predictive accuracy does not imply descriptive accuracy.

You will remember that an important assumption that is almost always made when a model is being built is the assumption of "ceteris paribus": that all variables other than those included in the model will remain unchanged. This does not mean that we really believe that other factors will remain unchanged, only that we do not expect them to have much effect on the variables in which we are interested. Again, the usefulness of this assumption must be judged by its results. You should notice that it is a necessary assumption to make if we are to divide the study of man into several disciplines. If we could not make this assumption, there would be no disciplines of sociology, economics, political science, psychology, or biology, because we would have to consider all these factors in all studies of human behavior. We would need only one discipline, called "man."

MODELS AND THEORIES

Models are often used to test the validity of theories. It will be shown that the factors affecting this use are related to those that condition the acceptance of an explanatory model.

A theory can be defined as either "A system of assumptions, accepted principles, and rules of procedure devised to analyze, predict, or otherwise explain the nature or behavior of a specified set of phenomena," or "systematically organized knowledge applicable in a relatively wide variety of circumstances."[2] The first definition could equally well define some types of models. This confusion reflects the current use of the terms "model" and "theory" in the social sciences. They are often used interchangeably, but we shall be using these terms with separate, well-defined meanings. In this book, a theory will be "an exposition of abstract principles"; a model will mean a system of relationships that apply the theory to a given situation in the real world.

In the physical sciences, the difference between models and theories is much easier to discern. Newton's four laws of motion produce a theory of movement in the physical world. The familiar construct of planetary movements in which the planets of the solar system move around the sun is the model that applies this theory to a particular situation.

Examples in the social sciences are harder to find. Utility analysis of consumer demand is a theory, while the application of this theory to the demand for a particular good is a model. This division between theories and models is less clear in the social sciences than in the physical sciences. Although one can speculate about it, the reason for this can only be given by philosophers of science. It may well be a result of the relative states of development of the social and the physical sciences. The physical sciences have a longer history and seem to have reached a higher stage of development. They are capable of forming generalizations of a type that has largely eluded social scientists. While the physical sciences have been able to generalize their models into theories, the social sciences are still at the stage of building models largely without being able to generalize them. The stage of development that the social sciences have reached

---

[2]*American Heritage Dictionary of the English Language.* William Morris, ed. Boston: American Heritage Publishing Co. and Houghton Mifflin Company, 1973.

> **Tycho Brahe, 1546–1601**
>
> Brahe belonged to the generation of astronomers that followed Copernicus. Even though he believed until the day he died that all the planets revolved around the earth, he made a great many accurate observations of planetary movements. He amassed a great deal of data that enabled Kepler to build his model of planets moving elliptically around the sun. This later led to Newton's laws of motion.

today could well be compared to that of physics at the time of Tycho Brahe.

It would be useful at this point to spell out the operational relationship between a theory and the models derived from it. Conceptually, the theory comes before the model. The theory is the system of generalizations that the models apply to different situations. Historically, however, models have appeared before the more general theories. Models have been developed to answer specific questions about particular situations; similarities between various models have led to the formulation of generalizations that have developed into theories.

We now have a new question. What is a good theory?

There is a substantial body of thought among philosophers of science that claims that theories can never be proved.[3] This argument claims that scientific inquiry should be directed toward the refutation of theories. The goal of scientific activity should be to produce testable propositions from theories; these propositions should be capable of being shown to be wrong. If they are not shown to be wrong, the theory has not been *confirmed,* since it may be possible in the future to produce a contradictory result. The most that one can say about such a theory is that it has not been refuted.

It now becomes clear that there is a close and important relationship between the testing of models and the testing of theories. The role of models is to produce testable propositions that can be used in turn to test theories. If these propo-

---

[3]See, for example, Karl Popper, *Conjectures and Refutations,* 3rd Edition, ch. 3. (London: Routledge and Kegan Paul, 1969.)

sitions are not shown to be wrong, there are two conclusions that can be drawn. First, the model has been shown to be useful in that situation. Second, since the theory has not yet been refuted, it will probably command more confidence for having successfully faced another test.

It should also be clear that there is a close connection between the acceptance of theories and the acceptance of explanatory models. The two constructs are indeed very much related. The functions of an explanatory model are closely related to the functions of a theory. Both constructs are concerned with fundamental causes, the difference being in the generality of their concern. Moreover, because of this connection, they are both extremely difficult to test. They can both be proved wrong, but neither can be proved correct.

Strictly speaking, this is the most that can be said about the acceptability of theories and of explanatory models. Yet it is clear that theories and explanatory models do become positively accepted by the scientific community and by society as a whole. How does this happen?

This question is part of the study of the history of scientific thought; here we can do no more than indicate some possible directions of inquiry. It seems likely that acceptance depends less on positive testing than on normative aspects of the social environment.[4] For example, we of the twentieth century are more likely to accept the explanation of the pattern of rainfall over mountains that is based on temperature, air pressure and so forth than the one that relies on rain gods. We find the first explanation more acceptable than the second not because the evidence is more convincing (few of us know what the evidence is) but rather because we live in a society that believes in "natural causes." An explanation in terms of Rain Gods is simply not emotionally satisfying for the people of our society.

There are obviously many other unanswered questions. What factors determine the social environment? How do they change? These questions and others would have to be examined before we could begin to discover why some theories are accepted and some are rejected, and why theories that are

---

[4]One should remember that the explanation of planetary movements in which the planets, including the earth, moved in ellipses around the sun was accepted before there was good evidence for it. The most convincing piece of evidence, the existence of parallax (the movement of the fixed stars), did not appear until much-improved telescopes were developed, which occurred after the explanation had already been accepted.

rejected by one generation are accepted unreservedly by the next.

MODIFICATION OF MODELS

What do we do when a predictive model has been tested and has been found wanting? We could, of course, discard the model and start again. This extreme step should only be taken when other attempts have failed, however. It is better to first try to modify the model.

First, it is useful to check the reasoning used to derive predictions from the model. This is simply a matter of checking the manipulation of the variables in the model; it has nothing to do with the model-building itself. Failures in reasoning *are*, however, one cause of wrong predictions.

The Quantity Theory

The Quantity Theory has had a long history in economic theory—it first appeared in the late eighteenth century. The basic idea behind it is that there is a stable relationship between the quantity of money in the economy (cash, checking accounts, and so forth) and the money value of output. More specifically, if the total volume of output remains the same, changes in the quantity of money will lead to changes in prices. (For example, increases in the quantity of money will cause inflation.) Recent work by Professor Milton Friedman at the University of Chicago and by many of his colleagues has built upon this simple idea to produce more sophisticated models of the way in which a modern economy behaves.

If the accuracy of the reasoning used in the model has been proved, wrong predictions can be traced to other factors. There are often problems in matching measurements of variables in the real world to those of their conceptual counterparts. Inaccurate predictions are often a result of this difficulty. Many of the discussions on the validity of the quantity theory have revolved around the empirical definition of money. Is "money" cash, cash and demand deposits, or cash, demand deposits, and time deposits? The predictions of models of the quantity theory depend crucially on the definition chosen.

Another source of failure in models is their assumptions. When models fail to predict accurately, one may decide to correct the assumptions. One of the most important in this case is likely to be "ceteris paribus." To increase the predictive accuracy of the model, it may be desirable to increase the number of variables.

If all attempts at modification fail, then one may be justified in discarding the model completely. This is really the same as modifying some postulates, thus changing one's view of the world. This strategy is reasonable if there is an alternative model to replace the one discarded. If there is no alternative, one has to decide whether a model that is less than totally satisfactory is better than no model at all. This question is important; its answer is essentially normative. One may decide that an unsatisfactory model is so misleading that it would be less dangerous to have no model at all. For example, it could be argued that governments that have used poor macroeconomic models have gotten worse results than those that had no model at all and left the economy alone. No general advice can be given about the rejection or acceptance of models; it is dependent both on the specific situation and on the personal values of the model user.

QUESTIONS

1. What positive and normative issues are involved in answering the question, "What is a good model?"

2. Review what is meant in this text by the terms "postulate," "assumption," "proposition," "prediction," and "forecasting."

3. Consider the following: "Marx's forecasts concerning the historical behavior of capitalism have been wrong, but the predictions derived from his basic model are correct." Is this a reasonable view of Marx's work on capitalistic economic crises?

4. Review the positive criteria for a satisfactory model.

5. What problems are involved in the evaluation of an "explanatory" model?

6. If you had to choose between two different predictive models of the same piece of reality, what stated and unstated tests would you apply?

7. How does a "theory" differ from a "model"?

8. One of the major problems in the testing of economic models is the extent to which the measurements of variables in the real world actually match those of their conceptual counterparts. The measurement of "money" for the purposes of testing the "quantity theory of money" involves problems of conceptualization, definition, and measurement. Can you identify other such problem areas in economics? Is the problem limited to the testing of economic models?

MATHEMATICAL TECHNIQUES

7

Angling may be said to be like the mathematics, that it can never be fully learned.

— Izaak Walton

Many students find the use of mathematical techniques intimidating and alienating. They feel that the models built upon them are far removed from the world in which they are interested. They are also often baffled by the use of techniques that they understand only imperfectly.

In spite of this, there is an increasing tendency to formulate economic models mathematically. Indeed, it is impossible to find an economics textbook written in the last twenty years that does not use some mathematical techniques. While most books include at least such fundamentals as graphs and elementary algebraic manipulations, many others use slightly more advanced skills, such as the solution of simultaneous equations and differential calculus. More advanced mathematical techniques may also be encountered.

It is the purpose of this chapter to discuss the reasons for the use of mathematical techniques in economics and to introduce students to some of those that are more widely used. It is our intention not to teach these techniques, but to indicate their role in economic analysis. References to suitable mathematics textbooks will be provided.

MATHEMATICS AS A LANGUAGE

In Chapter 2, we saw that descriptions made use of many different media, and that the medium chosen depended essentially upon the purpose of the description. It should also be clear that a description in one medium can usually be translated into another. For example, a photograph can be translated into a verbal description. When such a translation takes place, however, some of the advantages of the original are lost. A verbal description may present as accurate an account of a route through a city as a map; but this verbal description would not be as easy to use. We are so accustomed to using a map that it provides us with a more useful description of routes than any other type of description can. Yet in a culture unaccustomed to maps, this would not be true; in such cultures other types of description may be more useful. Thus, although it is possible to translate a description into other media, there are usually certain media that are especially suited for a particular purpose. Similar remarks can be made about predictive economic models.

Some economists would claim that, since mathematics is a language, all mathematical models can be expressed verbally, and all verbal models can be expressed mathematically.[1] Thus, there is essentially no difference between translating English to mathematics (or mathematics to English) and translating English to French (or French to English).

While it is formally true that the model is independent of the language in which it is formulated, the choice of this language is not trivial. Continuing the French-English analogy for the moment, it can be argued that one language is more useful for some purposes than for others. French is a more useful language for cooking, and English is more useful for technical conversations.[2] Although these specializations do not prohibit translation, they do cause some small difficulties. Similarly, economic models can be formulated either verbally or mathematically, but each method has its own advantages and disadvantages. Each language is more suitable for some purposes than for others.

There are basically three kinds of languages that have been used to formulate economic models. These are (a) ver-

---

[1] Paul A. Samuelson, "Economic Theory and Mathematics: An Appraisal." *American Economic Review*, Vol. XLII, No. 3. (June 1952.)

[2] Think of words and phrases such as sauté, crouton, and en cocotte. They have no direct counterparts in English but are so useful that they have an accepted English usage. If we wanted to use English words, we would have to replace each word or phrase by a longer phrase that defined it. Similarly, English has become the international language of civil aviation.

bal, (b) graphical, and (c) algebraic.[3] Their historical appearance has been roughly in this order. Early discussions of economics used only verbal reasoning. Graphs soon made their appearance, however, and Marshall's *Principles,* published in 1890, contained all three languages.[4] Most modern textbooks rely heavily on graphs, with some verbal formulations, while many of them also include a great deal of algebraic reasoning.

The language of mathematics has to be learned. This process has two aspects analogous to the learning of any other language — it is necessary to learn both its "vocabulary" and its "grammar."

The "vocabulary" of mathematics is mathematical notation, which often confuses and alienates non-mathematicians. We shall give a few common examples of mathematical notation and "translate" them into English. Whenever you encounter mathematical notations, you should make sure that you can translate them in this way until you become familiar with them.

EXAMPLES

Mathematics: $\therefore$
Read as: therefore

Mathematics: $y = f(x)$
Read as: y is a function of x
English: y is related to x in an unspecified manner

Mathematics: Δy
Read as: delta y
English: the change in the value of y

Mathematics: $\dfrac{dy}{dx}$
Read as: dy, dx
English: the change in the value of y that results from an infinitesimally small change in the value of x

---

[3]Algebraic reasoning includes simultaneous equations and differential calculus as well as many other techniques not considered here. Algebraic reasoning is simply reasoning with symbols by following certain rules of manipulation.

[4]Alfred Marshall, *Principles of Economics,* 8th ed. (London: Macmillan & Co., 1922.)

Mathematics:	$Q_d = a - bP$
Read as:	Qd is equal to a minus bP
English:	Q_d is equal to a minus b times P

Mathematics:	$P = \dfrac{a - c}{d + b}$
Read as:	P is equal to a minus c, all over d plus b
English:	P is equal to a minus c, all divided by the sum of d plus b

There are many other examples.

The "grammar" of mathematics is essentially the rules of manipulation. These rules include those for the solution of simultaneous equations, for the differentiation of a function, for arithmetic, and so forth.[5]

CHOICE OF LANGUAGE

Does the choice of language merely result from changing fashions, or are there specific criteria that can influence this choice?

We believe that, although there are no fixed rules about which language is most appropriate for the formulation of economic models, there are certain factors that should be considered when making this choice. There are four questions that should be asked of each language.

How Easy is it to Formulate a Particular Model in One Language Rather Than Another?

For a very large number of models, it is usually easier to formulate the model algebraically rather than verbally or

---

[5]Students who have little understanding of mathematical techniques will find the following three books very useful.

Michael Eraut, *Fundamentals of Arithmetic.* (New York: McGraw-Hill, 1970.)

Michael Eraut, *Fundamentals of Elementary Algebra.* (New York: McGraw-Hill, 1970.)

Michael Eraut, *Fundamentals of Intermediate Algebra.* (New York: McGraw-Hill, 1970.)

All three books are written in such a way as to avoid the duplication of material that is already understood.

Another useful book is: G. C. Archibald and Richard G. Lipsey, *An Introduction to a Mathematical Treatment of Economics,* 2nd edition. (London: Weidenfeld and Nicolson, 1973.) While useful as an introduction to calculus, this book assumes an understanding of algebraic techniques.

graphically. The algebraic method is usually more economical. It takes less time both to write and to read. For example, models that contain relationships between many variables are too long and complex when expressed in ordinary English. It is much easier to express such models in algebraic language.

For some models, however, there may be no algebraic techniques that are suitable. Before the invention of the symbolic form of a functional relationship, how could one possibly have represented algebraically a relationship between two variables whose specific relationship was unknown? Now, $y = f(x)$ means that y is related to x in some as yet unspecified manner. This relationship could not have been represented algebraically before the f notation was developed.

How Easy is it to Manipulate the Model in the Chosen Language?

It is easier to manipulate a model formulated graphically or algebraically than one formulated verbally. For example, consider a problem that can be analyzed by a model of supply and demand. What happens to the price of a good when a tax is levied on it?

The verbal analysis would be something like the following. Consumers will buy less of a good as the price rises; producers will produce more of the good only if the price rises; and the market price will be the price at which the amount of the good that consumers want to buy is equal to the amount that producers want to sell. If a tax is imposed, the cost of the good will be increased. Therefore, the price will rise, and consumers will want to buy a smaller amount.

With the verbal analysis, it is difficult to derive more precise predictions. We can simply predict the *directions* of changes; we cannot say anything about the *size* of the change.

Figure 7.1 shows the graphical analysis of this problem. P and Q are the price and the quantity, respectively, of the good concerned. DD is the demand curve, which shows the relationship between the price of the good and the amount of the good that consumers want to buy. SS is the supply curve, which shows the relationship between the price of the good and the amount of it that producers are willing to sell. S^1S^1 is the supply curve after the imposition of the tax; t is the

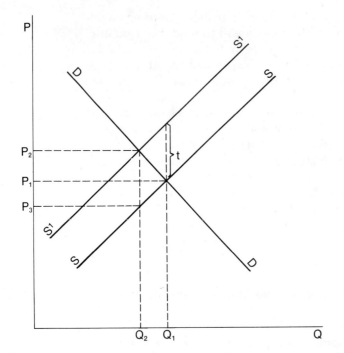

Figure 7–1.

amount of the tax on each unit of the good. P_1 is the price of the good before the tax, and q_1 is the amount bought and sold. After the tax, P_2 becomes the price and Q_2 the amount. It can be seen that P_2 is greater than P_1, but *the increase in price is less than the full amount of the tax.* Therefore, the price received by the producer is only P_3, which is less than P_1. Thus, the graphical analysis can tell us a little more about this problem than the verbal explanation could.

Now consider an algebraic formulation of the model. Let the demand curve be represented by the equation

$$Q_D = a - bP,$$

where Q_D is the quantity demanded, P is the price, a is the amount that would be bought if the price was zero, and b is the incremental demand for each unit decrease in price. Let the supply curve before the tax be represented by the equation

$$Q_s = c + dP,$$

where Q_s is the quantity supplied, P is the price, c is the amount supplied when the price is zero, and d is the incremental supply for each unit increase in price. For the original price, P_1, Q_D must equal S_s; therefore, P_1 can be found by solving the equation

$$a - bP = c + dP.$$

Rearranging this equation, we obtain

$$P = \frac{a - c}{d + b}$$

Now the supply curve after the imposition of the tax can be represented by the equation

$$Q_s = c + d(P - t),$$

where t is the tax per unit.
P_2 can be found by solving the equation

$$a - bP = c + d(P - t).$$

Rearranging this equation, we obtain

$$P = \frac{a - c + dt}{d + b}.$$

Now we know that

$$P_1 = \frac{a - c}{d + b}$$

and

$$P_2 = \frac{a - c + dt}{d + b}$$

and the increase in price is the difference between P_1 and P_2. This difference is

$$P_2 - P_1 = \frac{a - c + dt}{d + b} - \frac{a - c}{d + b}$$

$$\therefore P_2 - P_1 = \frac{dt}{d + b}.$$

Thus, the algebraic method tells us not only that the increase in price is less than the amount of the tax, but also that this increase is $\frac{dt}{d+b}$; that is, the increase depends on the tax and on the slopes of the demand and the supply curves (b and d).[6]

This example demonstrates the importance of formulating models algebraically if one is to be able to manipulate them to obtain precise predictions.

How Clear are the Assumptions of the Model?

Again, the algebraic formulation has advantages over the other methods. Although it is possible to make the assumptions of a verbal or a graphical model explicit, it is also possible to ignore the existence of some assumptions. Such an omission is less likely in an algebraic model, because each algebraic statement is clear and unambiguous. In our previous example, the equation

$$Q_D = a - bP$$

is explicitly making a statement about "ceteris paribus." The quantity demanded depends only on price, *all other things being equal*. Thus, the final statement about the change in price is true only if this assumption is a useful one to make in this situation. It is impossible to hide this assumption by saying "perhaps," as one can in a verbal formulation.

How Easy is it to Communicate the Model to Other People?

The answer to this question obviously depends largely on who the other people are. If they too are economists with an understanding of mathematical techniques, this question becomes redundant. One then has to consider the appropriate language only in terms of the other three criteria (formulation, manipulation, and assumptions). If it cannot be pre-

---

[6]We have already defined b and d as the incremental amounts demanded and supplied for a given unit change in price. If you look at Figure 7.1, you will see that this also defines the slopes of the demand and the supply curves.

sumed that the potential audience understands these techniques, however, then a verbal formulation will be necessary. Nevertheless, in most cases it will prove useful to formulate and manipulate the model mathematically, then translate the process into verbal reasoning. Serious mistakes in reasoning may then be avoided.

MATHEMATICAL LANGUAGES: STRENGTHS AND WEAKNESSES

Graphs

The use of graphs in economic analysis is now widespread. A graph shows visually the relationship between two variables. Figure 7.2 is a graph of a demand curve, DD, which expresses the relationship between the price of the good and the quantity that consumers will want to buy. This graph shows that at a price of $1 per unit, consumers will buy 700 units; at a price of $2 per unit, they will buy 550; and at a price of $3 per unit, they will buy 400.

The graphical representation has the advantage that it is easy to use and is visually stimulating. On the other hand, it has the disadvantage that only two or, in rare cases, three

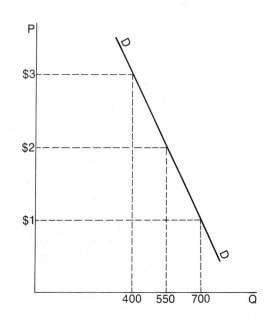

Figure 7–2.

variables can be represented on it.[7] It is frequently useful, however, to examine the behavior of two variables in isolation, in which case a graph can prove to be a very useful tool. In the field of international trade, for example, graphs have generated a powerful and influential body of theories. Nevertheless, their power has also to some extent been a disadvantage. The use of graphs has resulted in a proliferation of analyses of the trade of two goods between two countries that have two factors of production. The strong tradition of the use of graphs has meant that analyses of more general cases have been restricted.

Algebra

This limitation of graphs can be avoided by the use of algebra. Most graphs can be expressed by an algebraic equa-

---

[7]Some graphs can be developed that show many more than two variables; these graphs are used frequently in international trade theory. However, such graphs are still limited by the two-dimensional nature of the medium. They usually analyze trade between *two* countries with *two* factors of production producing *two* goods.

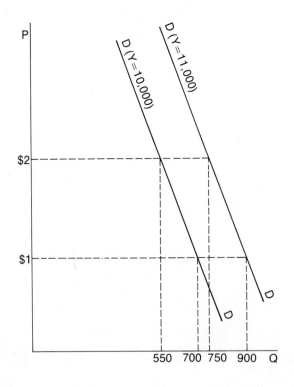

Figure 7–3.

tion. The graph shown in Figure 7.2 can be represented by the equation

$$Q_D = 850 - 150P.$$

(Translated: if the price of an item is 0, then consumers would like to have 850 units of it; as the price goes up by $1 per unit, consumers will buy 150 units less.) The equation gives us all the information contained on the graph and uses less space. Moreover, it can be extended to include a greater number of variables.

Suppose we knew that the quantity demanded also depended on the average income (Y) of the consumers. Figure 7.3 shows this new situation. $DD(Y = 10,000)$ shows the demand curve when average income is $10,000, while $DD(Y = 11,000)$ shows the demand curve when average income is $11,000. The graph is beginning to become quite crowded.

The same relationship can be represented algebraically by the equation[8]

$$Q_D = -1150 - 150P + \frac{1}{5} Y$$

and can be expanded by as many variables as proves necessary.

The preceding discussion is intended only to show that while graphs are useful, algebra is even more useful. More advanced algebraic techniques, in particular, the solution of simultaneous equations and differential calculus, are also excellent tools for economists.

Simultaneous Equations

In economic analysis, we are seldom interested in only one relationship. We are usually more interested in the interaction between two or more relationships such as supply and demand, saving and investment, imports and exports, and so forth. The solution of simultaneous equations proves to be very useful for these purposes.

---

[8]Translated: Quantity demanded depends both on the price of the product and on income. For each dollar increase in price, with income constant, consumers will want to buy 150 units less. For each dollar increase in income, consumers will want to buy one fifth of a unit more. When both price and income are zero, they want a negative amount—that is, they want to sell 1150 units of the amount that they already possess. This latter information is not even on the graph.

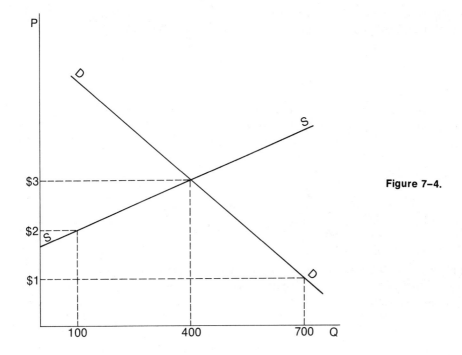

Figure 7–4.

Let us look again at the analysis of supply and demand. In Figure 7.4, *DD* is the demand curve already seen in previous examples. *SS* is the supply curve for the good. The market price will tend to move toward the price at which the quantities supplied and those demanded are equal. We can see from the graph that this price is $3 per unit and that the quantity supplied equals that demanded—400 units. Thus, the market price is the value at which the supply and demand curves intersect.

This price can also be found algebraically. The demand curve is given by the equation

$$Q_D = 850 - 150P,$$

and the supply curve is given by the equation

$$Q_s = -500 + 300P.$$

Now if we add the further condition that Q_D should be equal to Q_s, we have a pair of simultaneous equations to be solved. Simultaneous equations can be solved for any number of variables so long as there are a corresponding number of

equations. Generally, so long as the number of equations is equal to the number of unknown variables, all the variables can be found. The equations must be different, however. The two equations

$$2Q_s = 200 + 200 \text{ P}$$

and $$Q_s = 100 + 100 \text{ P}$$

cannot be solved because they are really the same equation. If drawn on a graph, the two lines would coincide. They would be the same line and therefore could not intersect.[9]

We have seen that simultaneous equations can be expressed and handled in two mathematical languages: graphs and algebra. Graphs can only be used for a system with two equations, however. A greater number of equations must be analyzed by using algebraic language.

Differential Calculus

Differential calculus is a mathematical technique concerned with changes in one variable that result from changes in another.[10] This technique has also proved very useful in economic analysis.

For example, consider the output decisions of a firm. Assume that the firm wishes to maximize its profits. How much should it produce?

The verbal argument reasons that the firm will continue to produce more output so long as each extra unit adds more to the company's revenue than to its costs. An extra unit that would add more to costs than to revenue will not be produced. If we call the addition to revenue of the extra unit "marginal revenue" and the addition to cost "marginal cost," then the firm will produce at that output at which marginal revenue is equal to marginal cost. This is the point of maximum profits. Further reasoning will tell us that for outputs less than the optimum, marginal revenue must be greater than marginal cost, and for outputs greater than the optimum, marginal revenue will be less than marginal cost. That is, for

---

[9]Students who doubt this should demonstrate it to themselves on graph paper.

[10]It can handle relationships between any number of variables, but in the example considered in the appendix to this chapter, we shall restrict ourselves to two variables.

outputs below the optimum, profits will increase when output is increased, because this will add more to revenue than to costs. Similarly, for outputs above the optimum, profits will be increased by reducing output, because this will reduce costs more than revenue.

Both conditions can be easily obtained by using differential calculus.[11]

Although both conditions can be obtained verbally, it is important for one to be able to use differential calculus. It has three distinct advantages over verbal reasoning.

First, it can cope easily with quite complex problems. The example in the appendix is relatively simple, but when the number of variables is increased, it becomes easier to handle the problem with calculus.

Second, once one is able to differentiate, it is easy for him to find the values of marginal revenue and marginal cost from the equations of the total amounts. Without differential calculus, it is necessary to calculate the value of revenue at an output of x and at $x + 1$, and then to subtract the first result from the second. This takes much longer than simply differentiating and then substituting the relevant values.

Third, the status of conditions such as "marginal revenue equaling marginal cost" becomes clearer. This condition follows directly from the assumption of profit maximization. There is no room for argument once profit maximization is assumed. "Marginal revenue equals marginal cost" is mathematics, not economics. Economic analysis is concerned with the variable that is to be maximized.

MATHEMATICAL MODELS AND ECONOMIC POLICY

Ideally, precise predictions should be used in the making of economic policy. It is useful to know how much of a good will be sold after the imposition of a tax so that the government can calculate the amount of revenue that it will receive. It is important to be able to predict the change in GNP resulting from a change in income tax rates. It is important to be able to predict the size of the change in oil exploration that would result from a given change in oil depletion allowances. There are many more examples.

Such predictions are virtually impossible to make unless mathematical models are built. We cannot insure precise

---

[11]See the appendix to this chapter.

predictions simply by building a mathematical model, however. For example, we may build a model in which we represent the demand curve by the equation

$$Q_D = a - bP,$$

but this alone will not yield precise predictions. We need to know the values of a and b. The discovery of these values will be the subject of the next chapter, but it would be well to admit now that this is no easy matter. Because of the complexity of economic phenomena and the paucity of economic data, the precise forms of relationships such as demand curves are very difficult to obtain.

Even though we may find it difficult to make the kind of predictions that would be desirable in an ideal world, this is no excuse for ignoring economic analysis or for refusing to build mathematical models. Our present aim should surely be to produce as precise a prediction as possible, even though we may only be able to produce predictions about the direction of change. At the same time we should endeavor to improve statistical and data gathering techniques to obtain more precise predictions.

A Word of Caution

There is little to be said in favor of the use of mathematics in economics *for its own sake*. Mathematics is a very useful tool, but it should not be confused with the real substance of economics. There is much good economic analysis that makes little or no use of mathematics;[12] conversely, there is an increasing tendency to build and manipulate elaborate mathematical models that contain little or no economics.

The combination of mathematics and economics can be extremely powerful, but it must always be remembered that mathematics is a valuable *servant* for the economist. It seems all too easy for mathematics to become the master. For example, problems may be chosen not for their economic interest, but because they provide an opportunity for the economist to demonstrate his mathematical prowess. This attitude can only bring into disrepute the use of mathematics by economists.

---

[12]For example: T. W. Schultz, *Transforming Traditional Agriculture.* (New Haven: Yale University Press, 1964.)

Appendix

Let R be total revenue, C total cost, P price, c unit cost, Π profits, and Q output. Assume that the demand and supply (cost) curves are the same as in the other examples in the chapter.

$$R = PQ$$

Price depends on output and can thus be obtained from the demand curve:

$$Q = 850 - 150P$$

$$\therefore P = 5\frac{2}{3} - \frac{Q}{150}$$

$$\therefore R = \frac{17}{3}Q - \frac{Q^2}{150}$$

From the supply curve,

$$Q = -500 + 300P$$
since $\qquad c = P,$
$$Q = -500 + 300c$$

$$\therefore c = \frac{Q}{300} + \frac{5}{3}$$

$$C = cQ$$

$$= \frac{Q^2}{300} + \frac{5}{3}Q$$

$$\Pi = R - C$$

$$= \frac{17}{3}Q - \frac{Q^2}{150} - \frac{Q^2}{300} - \frac{5Q}{3}$$

$$= \frac{12Q}{3} - \frac{3Q^2}{300}$$

$$= 4Q - \frac{Q^2}{100}$$

The problem is one of finding the maximum value of Π by changing Q. How does Π change as Q changes?

The symbol, $\dfrac{d\Pi}{dQ}$, represents a change in Π as a result of a change in Q and can be obtained by differential calculus.

$$\Pi = 4Q - \frac{Q^2}{100}$$

$$\therefore \frac{d\Pi}{dQ} = 4 - \frac{Q}{50}$$

Now Π is at a maximum or minimum when $\dfrac{d\Pi}{dQ}$ is equal to 0 because, at this point, Π is not increasing or decreasing as a result of changes in Q. Thus, when $\dfrac{d\Pi}{dQ} = 0$,

$$4 - \frac{Q}{50} = 0$$

$$\therefore \frac{Q}{50} = 4$$

$$\therefore Q = 200$$

This gives a maximum value for Π only if $\dfrac{d\Pi}{dQ}$ itself was decreasing as Q increased; that is, it is a point of maximum profits only if Π decreases with further increases in Q.

In the symbols of differential calculus, if $\dfrac{d^2\Pi}{dQ^2}$ is negative, then Π is at a maximum. In our example,

$$\frac{d^2\Pi}{dQ^2} = -\frac{1}{50}$$

and therefore $Q = 200$ gives maximum profits. What do these results mean in terms of marginal cost and marginal revenue?

$$\Pi = R - C$$

$$= \frac{17}{3}Q - \frac{Q^2}{150} - \frac{Q^2}{300} - \frac{5Q}{3}$$

$$\therefore \frac{d\Pi}{dQ} = \frac{17}{3} - \frac{2Q}{150} - \frac{Q}{150} - \frac{5}{3}$$

$$= \frac{dR}{dQ} - \frac{dC}{dQ}$$

Yet $\frac{dR}{dQ}$ and $\frac{dC}{dQ}$ are marginal revenue and marginal cost, respectively. Thus, when $\frac{d\Pi}{dQ} = 0$, marginal revenue is equal to marginal cost. Π is at a maximum only if $\frac{d^2\Pi}{dQ^2}$ is negative.

$$\frac{d^2\Pi}{dQ^2} = \frac{d^2R}{dQ^2} - \frac{d^2C}{dQ^2}$$

We can see that $\frac{d^2\Pi}{dQ^2}$ is negative only if $\frac{d^2R}{dQ^2}$ is less than $\frac{d^2C}{dQ^2}$; that is, if marginal revenue is increasing more slowly than marginal cost.

QUESTIONS

1. What alternative "languages" are available to us when we are formulating an economic model? What questions should we ask before deciding on the language to be used in any particular model? Would the answers to each question be different for a university research economist than for an economist working for the Federal Administration? Why?

2. Express the following in English (the definitions of these terms are those usually used in economic analysis):

   (a) $Qd = -1150 - 150P + \frac{1}{5}Y$

   (b) $Qs = 100 + 50P$

   (c) $C = f(Y)$

3. (a) Construct graphically the demand curve for a commodity, based on the following information:

Price	Quantity Demanded
1	50
2	40
3	30
4	20
5	10
6	0

Work out the equation for the demand curve of the commodity.
(b) Construct graphically the supply curve on the same graph, based on the following information:

Price	Quantity Supplied
1	0
2	10
3	20
4	30
5	40
6	50

What is the equilibrium point? Construct the equation for the supply curve and then calculate the equilibrium price.

4. Find the equilibrium price:

$$Qd = 160 - 30P$$
$$Qs = 70 + 5P$$

A tax of two units is applied. What will the increase in price be?

5. A football sells at $P. The demand for it in thousands of balls per month is given by the equation

$$X = \frac{80}{P} - 2.$$

Plot the demand curve and estimate the point at which demand becomes zero.

6. Why is the concept of a small change in the value of a function of such importance to economics?

7. Defining any necessary symbols, write in functional notation:

(a) The quantity of a good demanded is related in some unspecified way to the price of the good.

(b) The quantity of bathing suits sold daily in Atlantic City is a function of the average number of hours of sunshine recorded in the city.

(c) The market demand for tomatoes is influenced by the price of tomatoes, their size, shape and firmness, the tastes of consumers, and the level of consumer income.

MODELS AND STATISTICAL TECHNIQUES   8

More and more use is being made of statistical techniques in economic research. Statistical methods are used for classifying data, for providing descriptive information about data, and for making statements about total populations on the basis of some sample data. For the economist, some command of statistical operations is essential if he is to keep abreast of developments in the subject, especially if he wishes to make some contribution toward that development.

Statistics, like economics, suffers from a popular confusion about its nature and aims. Originally, "statists" (as the word suggests) accumulated information about the state, such as the size of national populations, the number of firms, and so forth. Later, particularly during the nineteenth century, more formal operations were discovered that enabled statistical investigation to move beyond the simple collection and description of data. Statistics today is a formal study that can be thought of as a division of applied mathematics with its own language. The term "statistic" is used now to refer to some quantity, such as the sample mean, calculated from sample data. A statistic in formal terms is neither a "fact" nor an original observation. In studying statistics, just as in mathematics, the student should get used to the language (the rules of manipulation and the notation) from the outset.

DESCRIPTIVE STATISTICS

One of the aims of statistical investigation is to describe the characteristics of a mass of data in terms of a few simple and appropriate numbers. For example, examination results could be provided as a list of numbers. Twelve students may have received the following scores:

$$50, 40, 65, 71, 32, 45, 58, 60, 49, 52, 65, 50$$

This list is not very informative as it stands. It would be useful to have some way in which to summarize these numbers. The mean, variance, and standard deviation are useful summary statistics.

The Mean: A Measure of Location

The mean (arithmetic average) of a set of numbers is the average of that set. It can be thought of as the number that best characterizes the whole set. It is found by adding all the individual values and then dividing this sum by the total number of values in the group. Thus, the mean of the twelve scores is:

$$\frac{50+40+65+71+32+45+58+60+49+52+65+50}{12} = \frac{637}{12} = 53.08$$

In general, if we denote the mean of the set of numbers X_i (where there are i numbers represented by the numbers X_1, X_2, X_3, and so forth) as $\overline{X}$, then:

$$\overline{X} = \sum_{i=1}^{} \frac{X_i}{n}$$

where $\sum_{i=1}^{} X$ means "the sum of all the numbers represented by X_1, X_2, and so on, up to and including X_n." Therefore, in the preceding example, $X_1 = 50$, $X_2 = 40$, $X_3 = 65$, $X_4 = 71$, $X_5 = 32$, $X_6 = 45$, $X_7 = 58$, $X_8 = 60$, $X_9 = 49$, $X_{10} = 52$, $X_{11} = 65$, $X_{12} = 50$, and $n = 12$.

Measures of Dispersion

The variance and the standard deviation are both measures of how the individual values are distributed around the mean. That is, they measure how much variation there is in these values. The variance is the mean of the squares of the difference from the mean. So if we denote the variance of the set of values X_i by $V(X)$, then:

$$V(X) = \frac{\sum_{i=1}^{} (\overline{X} - X_i)^2}{n}.$$

The square of the differences is used because squares are always positive. If unsquared amounts were used, the negative amounts resulting from values above the mean would cancel the positive amounts resulting from values below it. In our example, the variance is 116.24. The standard deviation is the square root of the variance, in this case 10.78, and measures the *average* difference from the mean. (Some values will be farther from the mean, while others will be closer to it.)

By using the mean and the standard deviation, we now have two figures instead of twelve to describe the examination results. This gives us a convenient descriptive model for the entire range of results. Such elementary processes are not usually described as statistical models, but, in terms of the argument developed in this book, the use of the term is clearly justified in this situation. Descriptive statistics of this sort are primarily concerned with the classification and the description of data. Like description, descriptive statistics can be ends in themselves. We are usually more interested in inferential statistics, however;[1] that is, we are usually more interested in making statements about a total population on the basis of a sample drawn from that population.[2]

---

[1] A good introduction to elementary statistics, both descriptive and inferential, can be found in K. A. Yeomans, *Applied Statistics: Statistics for the Social Scientist.* Penguin Education X6, Studies in Applied Statistics, Vols. 1 and 2. (Harmondsworth, England: Penguin Books, 1968.)

[2] A "population" for statistical purposes is not necessarily composed of people. It is the total number of objects in which the statistician is interested.

INFERENTIAL STATISTICS

The concept of sampling is basic to inferential statistics. If we wish to arrive at reliable estimates about the characteristics of a certain total population that is too large to study in full (if, for example, we wish to discover the degree of association between consumer spending and income, but we cannot ask every family in the country about its spending habits), then we must look at the characteristics of a random sample of that population. The sample must be selected on a random basis for us to be reasonably sure that we are not studying a subsection of the population with non-typical behavior. Of course, there may be situations in which it is impossible to be sure that the data is, in fact, a random sample—for example, when making use of data collected by another researcher. In such situations, we may have no choice but to treat the data as a random sample; the conclusions should be drawn with care, however.

When first introduced to statistical work, students in economics often fail to see any connection between performing conceptual (or real) experiments with games of chance and the economic data with which they hope to be ultimately concerned. The connection is close and important, however. The concepts used in games of chance concern the probability of the occurrence of certain events. Since all models are probabilistic, such concepts are crucial to the testing of models. We want to know the probability of our model's being correct.

Probability and Probability Distributions

Uncertainty arises when an event has more than one outcome. If we wish to establish which event is more (or most) likely in a situation for which there is more than one possible result, then we must make probability statements.[3] Making a probability statement is essentially the same as placing a bet on the occurrence of some event. Stating that an event has a probability of happening of 25 per cent would be the same as accepting as fair a bet with the odds of 4 to 1. This is also the

---

[3]Peter H. Kermel and M. Polasek, *Applied Statistics for Economists*, 3rd ed. (London: Pitmans, 1970) Chapter 6, pp. 80–114, contains a useful treatment of probability and probability distributions.

Number of ball	Probability of Selection
1	1/10
2	1/10
3	1/10
4	1/10
5	1/10
6	1/10
7	1/10
8	1/10
9	1/10
10	1/10

same as saying that, if the situation is repeated, the event will occur an average of one out of every four times, or 25 per cent of the time.

A probability distribution is based on this idea. Suppose we are involved in an experiment that consists of removing at random balls from a bag containing ten numbered balls. If we replace the selected ball after each trial, then each ball has an equal chance of being selected at the next stage. We can now draw up a table that shows the probability of selection for each ball. Note that the sum of all these probabilities is equal to one; that is, one of the balls *must* be chosen each time.

Such a table describes a probability distribution because it shows the distribution of the probabilities of each event occurring. This probability distribution can also be drawn on a graph, as depicted in Figure 8.1. Each point shows the probability of selecting that particular ball. This kind of distribution is called a rectangular probability distribution (for obvious reasons). Its shape is a result of each event's having an equal probability of occurrence. The world is not usually like this, however. More complex probability distributions are usually encountered.

Suppose we have a room to be measured, and we already know its dimensions. If we organize a number of people to measure the room, we should not expect each person to produce results exactly equal to the known dimensions of the room. Most people would get the measurement approximately correct, but errors would creep in. Small differences would result from some people holding the tape more tautly than others, the sizes of their thumbs, differences in their dexterity, and so forth. The most likely result would be a set

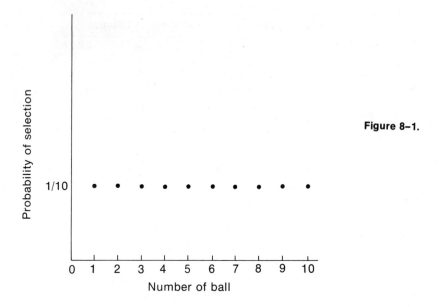

Figure 8–1.

of observations regularly distributed around a central value. In other words, the distribution of results will correspond to the type of probability distribution drawn in Figure 8.2. A curve of this general type (bell-shaped, continuous, and symmetrical) is known as the *normal probability curve*. This kind of probability distribution is very common, because large

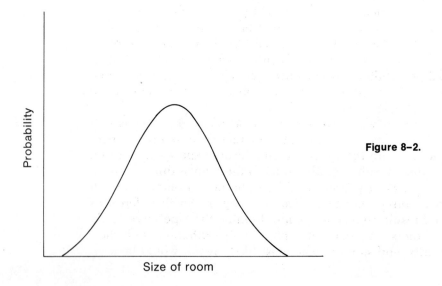

Figure 8–2.

Figure 8–3.

deviations from a central tendency are less common than small deviations. The probability distributions of height, weight, intelligence, and other personal characteristics have this shape.

There are many possible normal curves, but each normal curve is completely specified by its mean and its standard deviation. "Normality" refers to the shape of the curve and to the characteristics of that shape (bell-shaped, symmetrical, and asymptotic[4]), but the height and the spread of any partic-

---

[4]An asymptotic curve is one that approaches a given value but never quite reaches it.

Figure 8–4.

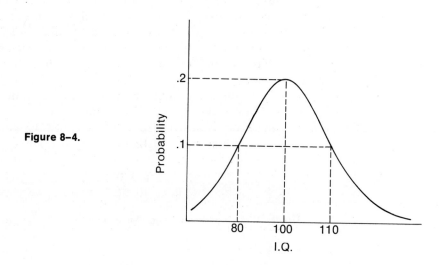

ular curve is determined by its mean and its standard deviation, respectively. Figure 8.3 shows a situation with two normal curves of the same mean but with different standard deviations.

If the events in a sample are distributed normally, it is possible to calculate the probability of obtaining a specific value. Suppose that intelligence measured by some kind of I.Q. test is distributed normally, as shown in Figure 8.4. We can see that if we pick someone at random, the probability of his having an I.Q. of exactly 100 would be .2 (if we pick many people, 20 per cent would have an I.Q. of 100). There is a probability of .1 of picking a person with an I.Q. of exactly 80 or of exactly 120. The probability of the person's having an I.Q. between 80 and 120 is the sum of the probabilities of all the values of I.Q. between 80 and 120. This concept of the probability of picking one event at random out of a total population is crucial for significance testing.

Significance Tests

When working with sample data, one may calculate a sample mean, $\overline{X}$. This sample mean may differ from the mean, μ, of the original population from which the sample was drawn.[5] This gives rise to two questions: What confidence can we have that the sample mean is the same as the mean of the population? If we have two samples, how much confidence can we have that they are derived from the same population? These two questions are the hub of significance testing and provide the basis for most statistical work. In effect, they are asking how much we can say about the population on the basis of a sample. If we take two samples and find that their means are different, we need to know the probability that they have come from the same population. If this probability is small, then we shall reject the hypothesis that they do come from the same population. The question immediately arises: How small is small? Putting it another way, "How much inaccuracy are we prepared to accept?" Generally, the answer in statistical investigation has been five per cent. The choice is arbitrary: It is a matter of judgment that has been embodied in statistical practice. We have come to

---

[5] μ is a Greek letter, pronounced mu, that is often used to denote the mean of the original population.

accept this five per cent probability of having wrongly rejected the hypothesis.

Regression and Correlation

So far the discussion has been concerned with only one variable. Economic analysis is rarely concerned with single-variable situations. For example, in the study of factors influencing the amount of gasoline sold at a service station, there are a number of factors that might be important. Some of these factors may be the number of hours it is open, the number of pumps, the number of service lanes, the price of gasoline, and so forth. A statistical model that relates these different aspects to the quantity of gasoline sold is required.

Regression and correlation analysis has been developed to deal with the relationships among a number of variables. In elementary situations, the regression analysis is concerned with the relationship between two variables, and the model used is sometimes called the two-variable linear model. The treatment of regression and correlation provided here is impressionistic; it is approached through a series of questions that attempt to do no more than point out the basic framework of the analysis. Models dealing with the relationships among many variables use similar, though more complicated, techniques.

Suppose we are dealing with a problem in which there are only two variables. We begin with a number of paired observations (such as profit and turnover in a service station). Our interest is in actually investigating the relationships between these two variables. Let us call these variables X and Y.

The first question that we would normally ask is, *"Is there any relationship between the two variables?"* We can draw the pairs of values on a scatter diagram to establish in visual form some idea of the distribution of the observations. Several possible types of scatter diagrams are shown in Figure 8.5. The next question is directly related to the first and is also straightforward: *"What kind of general relationship exists between the variables?"* Figure 8.5a shows a relationship that is positive and linear, though not perfectly so.[6] Fig-

---

[6] Strictly speaking, all that can be said from scatter diagram 8.5a is that the relationship is likely to prove positive and linear. This is, as X increases, Y appears to be increasing at a constant rate.

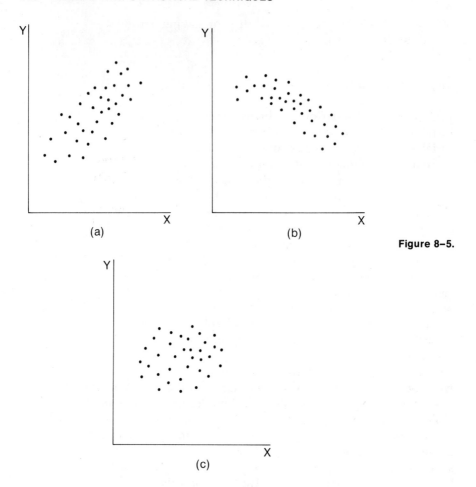

Figure 8–5.

ure 8.5*b* illustrates a relationship that is likely to prove nega-tive and linear; that is, a relationship in which the value of *Y* decreases as the value of *X* increases. Figure 8.5*c* indicates a situation in which there is no obvious relationship at first sight.

The basic pattern has now been tentatively established. The next question is, *"Can we specify the relationship in greater detail by fitting a trend line?"* Looking at the scatter diagrams, we might be tempted to believe that a trend line could be established simply by inspection; that is, by looking at the scatter of points and then attempting to draw in a straight line by hand. From elementary algebra we know that $Y = MX + C$ is the general equation of a straight line; *M* meas-ures the slope of the line, and *C* is the value of *Y* at which the line traverses the Y axis. If various people were asked to draw in the "best fitting line," some would undoubtedly get a good estimate for M and a poor estimate for C, while for others the reverse would be true. Whatever the outcome, it is unlikely that both the slope and the Y intercept would be estimated accurately enough to satisfy the statistician. We would still have to attempt to specify the nature of the relationship embodied in the line if we wanted to make use of the relationship for predictive purposes. A stricter method of establishing the slope and the intercept is needed.

We are attempting to fit the best possible line for the scatter points with which we are concerned so that we will be able to predict the actual values of Y, given the values of X. From the equation of a straight line, we know that for any actual straight line, the exact value of Y can be derived from that equation. Since we are unlikely to obtain a perfect fit of the mathematical results to the observed values, we normally try to derive a computed value for Y. The fitting of the trend line might then be seen as the answer to yet another question, which is, *"On the average, what value of Y is associated with a specified value of X?"* We are therefore concerned with getting the best possible estimate of Y for stated values of X. Intuitively, we would expect the process of obtaining such a line to be concerned with reducing the distances between the best fitting line and the actual observations. We would expect the distances between individual points and the best fitting line to be close overall. In fact, we would like the distance from all points to the fitted line to be as small as possible. We would like to find a line for which the sum of the differences of actual Y values from computed Y values is a minimum. The best fitting line is that line for which the sum of the squares of the vertical distance from the computed points to the actual points is a minimum.[7] For obvious reasons, this is called the *least squares method,* and the line found in this way is called the *regression line.* The regression equation is a measure of the average relationship between the variables, such that for any given value of X, we can predict a value for Y.

This leads us to another set of questions. The first is clearly, *"How good is the estimate, on the average?"* To put

---

[7]Remember that the statistician does not use unsquared values, because if he did, positive and negative values would cancel out. Values are squared to make them all positive. The procedure involved should be familiar to students who are already acquainted with the calculation of standard deviation.

it another way, "How close is the relationship?" This question takes us into a discussion of the coefficient of correlation.

The Coefficient of Correlation

The coefficient of correlation is a measure of the strength of the relationship between two variables. To get a clearer idea about what is meant by correlation, let us return to the original scatter diagrams.

Where the clustering of points around the trend line is "close," this represents a fairly high degree of correlation. Where the general location of points around the trend line is not close, this represents a low degree of correlation. How close is "close" is once again a matter of individual judgment.

Another way of looking at correlation is by returning to the formal problem faced in regression analysis. A best fitting line has been fitted to a series of points by means of the least squares method. Any point on this line is only a computed point; The actual value of Y may be above or below the computed point. The difference between the actual value of Y and the computed value of Y (that is, the value on the best fitting line) can be thought of as being "unexplained" by the regression. The better the fit, the smaller the gap between the "explained" value of Y and the actual value of Y. The observed values of Y vary; and some of this variation is explained by variations in X. The coefficient of correlation is computed from equations that look at the ratio between the variation of Y explained by X and the total variation of Y. The coefficient of correlation, usually denoted by the symbol r, merely indicates the closeness of this association. The formula is designed so that it will result in a value of 0 for perfectly unrelated variables and in a value of 1 for perfectly related variables.

The next question cannot be answered in such a straightforward manner. The question is, *"How confident are we that, in undertaking regression and correlation analysis, we have identified a real relationship?"* There are several aspects to this question. Seen one way, it is a question about the probability of obtaining a linear relationship with a high r value from a sample by chance. The question then becomes, "What is the probability that the random sample used as the basis for the selection of paired values could produce a relationship in the sample that does not exist in the total popula-

tion?" We are then back to the problem of significance testing, complicated by the fact that we are dealing with two
variables rather than one.[8]

The second aspect of the question is concerned with the
appropriateness of a two-variable model. It is to this problem
that we must now turn.

Causation, Correlation and the Meaning of r

In dealing with particular correlations, we must be careful how we interpret a high value of r. The correlation coefficient shows the degree of relationship between two variables. It does not in any way provide information about the
causal relationship between the variables. For instance, if we
find a high correlation between two variables, A and B, we
cannot say that A causes B, or that B is the cause of A. Tech-
nically, correlation implies only covariation. To move from a
high correlation to causation would require careful scrutiny
of the original data to detect other possible influences acting
on the independent variable. In the two-variable situation, it
might well be that both variables are related to a third. Thus,
the first two are highly related to each other, but changes in
one would not *cause* changes in the other in the real world.

We must be sure of several things before we can approach the idea of causation. First, we must be sure of the
original data: It should measure what we want it to measure.[9]
Second, we must be sure that the basic theoretical justification for looking at the relationship is convincing. Third, we
must be aware of the limitations of the two-variable model.

Let us take a situation in which we have a value for r that
is close to zero. When we are faced with this situation, it is
unwise to jump to the conclusion that there is no association.
All that we are justified in saying (subject to the condition of
applying a significance test) is that there is no linear relationship, although there may well be a curvilinear one.[10] As
well as providing the framework for the series of questions

---

[8]For an explanation of significance testing in these circumstances, see
Taro Yamane, *Statistics; An Introductory Analysis.* (New York: Harper &
Row, 1964.)

[9]This may seem to be a trivial point. As we noted earlier, however, many
social science data are difficult to observe directly, and so substitutes are often
used.

[10]Curvilinear simply describes a line that is not straight—a curved line.

asked above, a scatter diagram might also give us some idea of the likelihood of some other type of relationship existing.

As to the appropriateness of the two-variable model, it would be a mistake to look for uses for it in situations in which the basic relationships are more complex; for example, in the "explanation" of the volume of gasoline sales.

Having established the idea of investigating the appropriateness of the basic two-variable model and the "rightness" of the basic relationship being investigated (to avoid relationships that are only statistical with no theoretical justification), we must now return to the idea of causation. For example, take the economic analysis of education. Early in the development of economic analysis in this area, correlation analysis was used to look at the relationship between some measure of economic development (*GNP* per head) and some measure of education (elementary literacy, enrollment ratios, and so forth) in different countries. Usually, a positive linear relationship was established.

In dealing with these relationships, economists encountered problems with the data. Definitions of terms such as literacy differed from country to country. Second, the statistical analysis established a relationship only between increased levels of education and increases in GNP. It did not say that increased levels of education caused increases in GNP. It could be possible that, at higher levels of GNP, individuals are willing to consume more education. From the correlation analysis, both points could be argued.

We tend to expect increased GNP to result from specialization, the growth of human capital, increased understanding of market opportunities, or new techniques of production. Thus, benefits related to the growth of GNP may be expected from higher levels of education. This use of theory helps us to understand why, in the literature, we find economists explicitly recognizing that correlation does not prove causation, while at the same time they are using causality in putting their correlations to practical use. In dealing with the statistical model, we use both our knowledge of economics and our judgment. Judgment is essential, because it is possible to suggest that education is a good for which a high positive income elasticity of demand exists. If we accept this, then we would tend to argue for the opposite *causation*, but it would be *causation* that we would tend to see as economists rather than covariation. Caution is undoubtedly needed, but it seems that the note of caution normally struck is inconsistent with actual practice.

The conventional approach places strong emphasis on the need to avoid false correlations and the need to be sure that we are dealing with a real relationship. The fact that economists frequently make causal statements from correlations means that they are satisfied with the correctness of the underlying theoretical model. Others, of course, may not be so sure.[11] Judgment is involved here as in all other modeling situations.

---

[11]For an interesting treatment of correlation and causation, see M. Blaug, *An Introduction to the Economics of Education.* (London: Lane [Allen], 1970.)

Appendix

An interesting debate in the economics literature on the use and misuse of statistical techniques occurred in the 1920's. It concerned the derivation of statistical demand curves.[12]

A researcher interested in demand and supply analysis claimed that the statistical demand curve derived for pig iron predicted that, the greater the quantity of pig iron sold, the greater the price. Moore (the researcher in question) went on to claim that, not only did this statistical demand curve *refute* the accepted theory of supply and demand, but the statistical demand curve was also dynamic, whereas conventional theory was static.

E. J. Working, disturbed by the implications of Moore's remarks, set out to examine the nature of the statistical demand curve. He started by outlining the construction of statistical demand curves, and then he looked at the theory of supply and demand. Having looked at theory, he then re-examined the statistical demand curves.

The Construction of Statistical Demand Curves. The data are lists of actual prices and of the amount of pig iron sold at those prices over a period of time. Corrections are made to the data by using an index of the general level of prices over the time period in question.

Conventional Theory. Conventional theory states that a market is divided between buyers and sellers. The higher the price, the less that buyers wish to purchase and the more that sellers want to sell. Actual prices and quantities sold are determined by the intersection of the supply and the demand curves (the familiar supply and demand diagram). The model actually developed depends on other specified factors being constant, such as the level of income of the consumers. Changes over a period of time are then determined by shifts in the demand or supply curves.

Statistical Analysis in the Light of Economic Theory. If

---

[12]E. J. Working, "What do Statistical Demand Curves Show?" *Quarterly Journal of Economics*, Vol. 41 (1927), pp. 212–225.

statistical demand curves are constructed from observations of quantities sold at corresponding prices, then in terms of elementary theory, they are constructed from observations that tend to correspond to equilibrium points. In other words, the statistical demand curves drawn on this basis do not indicate the influence of demand any more than that of supply, because other things are not remaining unchanged.

Working does not totally reject statistical demand curves; he sees their importance in tracing out market developments. He does, however, stress the importance of caution so far as the statistical investigation of supply and demand is concerned. Specifically, he says: "As with the results of all other statistical analysis, statistical demand curves must be interpreted in the light of the original data and the methods of analysis used."

This excellent advice should be recalled whenever statistical techniques are used.

QUESTIONS

1. Read the following statistical notations in English:

   (a) $\overline{X}$ (b) Σx (c) $\overline{X} = \sum_{i=1}^{n} \frac{X_i}{n}$

2. What is meant by a probability distribution? What probability distributions do you know?

3. What are the general characteristics of the normal probability curve? Why is the curve so useful in statistical investigations?

4. Considering the probability of the following events, say which odds would be given by a bookmaker in taking bets for the events.

   Event A: probability of 25%

   Event B: probability of 10%

   Event C: probability of $12\frac{1}{2}\%$

5. How would you help your mother to arrive at a conceptual understanding of regression and correlation analysis?

6. What is normally meant by causation? What are the problems inherent in interpreting correlation as causation? Why do you think social

scientists frequently use high correlations as justifications for making causal statements?

7. Examine the following pairs of examples, and say whether you would be willing to investigate the relationships implied.

(a) The importation of Scotch whiskey and the size of Presbyterian communities in the Southern States.

(b) The output of the steel industry and the number of workers in the industry.

(c) Order of birth and mathematical ability.

(d) The output from technical schools and the level of per capita income in developing countries.

(e) Average weight of American football players per team and total league successes.

SCIENCE AND ART

9

Throughout this book, we have discussed the importance of judgment and imagination in the development and the interpretation of models. These ideas have been related to specific aspects of model-building and have therefore been isolated within particular contexts. The issue is of more general importance, however; it is related to the concept of economics as a science and to the general distinction and interrelationships between Science and Art. In this chapter, we shall discuss this last point more explicitly.

MODELS, JUDGMENT, AND IMAGINATION: A REVIEW

Many people are against the whole idea of models on the grounds that human behavior cannot be pressed into the simplifying molds of standard economic theory. The presentation of a variety of descriptions should have helped us to see, however, that inherent in *any* thoughtful statement about conditions in the "real world" is a sense of order and of relationships that makes simplification essential.

Building and using models is more than a simple mechanical process. In terms of the definition developed in Chapter 1, sheet music is a model for the reproduction of a particular melody. Yet the sheet music is not the entire model; other information must be brought to bear upon the model before the music will come alive. The musician needs to know the symbols and the instrument. Furthermore, he needs to develop some sort of relationship with the music in order to bring out different aspects of the score. This process of interpretation gives the particular piece its individuality and its life. The final creation is a mixture of straightforward interpretation (that is, understanding the symbols and playing the notes on a particular instrument for which the technical nature and limitations are understood) and imagination.

Language itself is a model. It is used to build relationships, as it was in the discussion about the advantages and the disadvantages of English and mathematics as scientific languages. The evolution of language is an exercise in modeling. The relationship between "trees" and "oak," "pine," "elm," and so forth is one in which "oak" is classified as a "tree," and therefore similar to "elm" but different from "grass." Yet "tree" and "grass" are also "vegetation." Anyone who has watched the development of a very young child from the stage of making baby noises to saying the first words in a recognizable language will be able to appreciate the effort that goes into establishing these very simple types of linguistic relationships. A child must learn to make both the sound and the sense clear.

Of course, the fact that there is an association in one person's mind between "tree" the word, "tree" the thing, and "tree" the idea does not guarantee that there are similar associations in another's. Normally, we act as if the meaning and the associations were clear to all concerned. The facts that imagination and language are closely related and that there is room for doubt may make experimentation and further extension of ideas and meanings possible.

Chapter 2, which dealt with the process of description, was essentially concerned with different types of language. Mailer wrote in English, and the statistician who compiled the list of figures about Chicago worked in the language of a particular kind of classification. Probably even before the basic data were collected, the statistical classification had to be specified and approved. The creative aspect of Mailer's work cannot be analyzed by *scientific* models, although those concerned with literary criticism are quick to identify patterns and themes in the writings of others. Literary critics search for models that will help in the classification and, ultimately, in the interpretation of literary works.

Laymen may not usually think of creative writing as a modeling process, but it involves the selection of themes to be explored (the questions), the methods to be followed (the genre, which is equivalent to the various classifications mentioned in Chapter 4), and the situations to be confronted (the data). We see the literary process primarily as an exercise in imagination. (Perhaps we should recall the definition of poetry as being ten per cent inspiration and ninety per cent perspiration.) Literary criticism is, however, at least implicitly carried out in this way. Furthermore, writers have organized into particular schools by self-selection (for example, the Bloomsbury Group, the Dadaists). This suggests not only that the style of approach is capable of being understood in terms of the modeling process (Romanticism, Naturalism, and so forth), but also that their areas of concern are of specific types, such as would be expected from a particular set of models.

The models are, of course, loose and vaguely specified, and we are not normally concerned with identifying them. Imagination no doubt predominates, but this does not preclude modeling. Similarly, even in very formal scientific models, imagination has a role to play. We saw in Chapter 2 the need for imagination in arriving at new classifications. (The example we gave was the fictitious one of big feet and small feet revealing patterns in the math scores of a class of students.) Imagination also plays a part in the development and the testing of particular models. Keynes needed a certain amount of imagination to invent not the *answers* to a new question (it could be argued that he never really answered his own question), but the new *question* itself.

In addition, models have interpretive rules. These rules are never formalized in economic analysis; at least, you will never find a list of rules that state how a model should be interpreted. Nevertheless, in listening to a good economist, you will become aware that you are hearing implications being drawn from a very simple model, and you may wonder why you did not see these implications yourself. The experienced economist will call upon both his imagination and his experience after building a particular model. Experience and imagination also play a part in laying the foundations of the model (specifying questions, classifying, and so forth) and in judging the significance of its results.

Models are essential to serious thought. They are used because people interpret the world by building up relationships. We have now added a new element—imagination—which is important for scientific analysis as well as for creative writing. Unlike the very loose models used by the creative artist, models in economic analysis are made to serve very specific purposes. The question that particular model explores is usually well defined, while the work of the creative writer may be concerned with a number of themes and their inter-relationships.

Economic models are—or should be—specific in two senses. They should be specific in the sense that the question being explored is clearly identified. Second (directly related to the first point), they are expected to produce clearly defined predictions. Sometimes we may succeed in specifying the appropriate question for a particular situation but may fail to explore the question adequately. It is for this reason that the list of motives for constructing economic models contained elements other than prediction. These other motives were listed as (a) description, (b) explanation, and (c) understanding.

In singling out prediction as the most important aspect of scientific models, certain points must be noted. First, almost any stand taken in economic analysis has ethical implications. The sorts of questions that an economist concerned with economic development will ask depend partly on his emotional identification with the problems he is facing. In building models, however, he will usually be forced to make his value judgments clear, and he should attempt to specify the questions so that they can be tested.

Second, there are limitations imposed by the types of models we build. It is not enough to argue that it is possible to change the model if it omits too many details because of limitations of the medium. The analogy of scales lies behind the idea of equilibrium; equilibrium models inhibit the analysis of disequilibrium processes. Because the equilibrium framework has been so useful, economists are finding it difficult to break out of this mold and develop disequilibrium models. Chapters 2 and 4 explored the limitations imposed by the "state of the arts."

Some element of bias may also be present in dealing with the predictions of positive economics. The market for automobiles seems to be far from perfectly competitive, yet we may wish to consider it as such for the analysis of certain questions—for example, the effects of an import tax on automobiles. We are saying here that the market behaves as if it were perfectly competitive, but we would not be correct in deriving welfare propositions from this model, because we are not using a model that says that the market is in fact perfectly competitive. It is not wrong to use the model of perfect competition to analyze an imperfect market if this model will answer the questions in which we are interested. It *is* wrong, however, to infer welfare consequences based on perfect competition when another sort of classification may be more appropriate.

SCIENCE AND ART

It should now be clear that there is some connection between the practice of Science and that of Art. Science makes use of imagination, which is usually thought of as an artistic characteristic, while artists use models (at least implicitly), which we have discussed in this book as being essential tools of the scientist. So it is useful or necessary to make a distinction between Science and Art? We would argue that it is.

The main distinction between Science and Art must surely be the intended end-product of each. Scientists intend to produce enlightenment (that is, increased knowledge about the world), while artists attempt to create a new and pleasing object. Great artists and great scientists do both, however; so this distinction refers only to end-products. Jane Austen, a great artist, produced not only entertaining, witty, and creative novels, but also a picture (a model) of social relationships in nineteenth century Britain. Charles Darwin, a great scientist, not only produced a scientific theory, but also had the creativity to produce a new view of the world in which man was seen as another animal instead of as a separate creation, as he had been thought to be earlier.

Why are we, as economists, interested in the differentiation and the relationship between Science and Art? The answer is essentially historical. In universities, the study of economics has been carried out in Arts faculties, and this historical accident has affected the way in which economics has been viewed. The importance of using scientific methods—that is, producing predictions and testing them against the facts—has not been universally accepted. Indeed, this book is itself part of a considerable literature seeking to defend the use of scientific methods in the study of economics.

John Stuart Mill defined Science as a body of truth and Art as a set of rules founded upon Science.[1] By this, he meant that

---

[1]John Stuart Mill, *Essays on Some Unsettled Questions on Political Economy.* (London: John W. Parker, 1844.)

the development of economic policy (an art) was based upon truths about the economic system discovered by science. We have seen that the situation is more complex than that, however. The formulation of appropriate questions, the establishment of appropriate classifications, and the adoption of suitable ways of answering the questions all involve judgment. The predictions derived from other models help by suggesting useful classifications or by identifying new questions. When a prediction is derived from a model, the question of interpretation remains. The model is not the real world, and we cannot be certain that the process in the model is similar to the process being examined in the real world. Judgment is again involved in relating the predictions derived from the model to reality. This stage is not usually taught in a straightforward manner; we are supposed to pick it up as we go along. This process of getting from the model to the real world involves interpretive rules. These rules are in fact an art involving skill, judgment, and economic understanding.

The natural sciences do not at this time face serious problems in forming questions, establishing relationships, and so forth. Evolutionists still run into ethical objections from those who believe in the revelation of the Bible. Yet with one or two important exceptions, the natural sciences are able to avoid normative questions.

In contrast, ideology has played an important role in the formulation of questions and the construction of classifications in the social sciences. The language of "social class" is filled with value judgments, as is the study of "enterprise." In the literature of economic development, there has been little general agreement on the terms to be used for certain countries. There have been objections to "underdeveloped" on ethical grounds and to "developing" on both positive and normative grounds. There are numerous people in the Third World who object to the suggestion of rank in these terms.

The natural sciences are in a much better position when it comes to normative questions. The question, "Should the earth go around the sun?" has no meaning today; whereas the question, "Should the distribution of income be more equal?" does have important meaning. Researchers in the natural sciences still must face normative questions from time to time, however. The more scientific research into the maintenance of human life is conducted, the greater are the number of ethical questions that scientists must face. Whether a human being has in fact died is now largely a matter of judgment. Owing to the scientific equipment now available, "life" and "death" must be redefined.

In dealing with the development of any discipline, the classifications we use and the questions we ask are of great importance. The historical ingredient in economics cannot be ignored.[2] At certain points in history, particular questions have emerged as being important. This does not mean that all research into economic phenomena is dominated by current concerns. Much research arises from a simple desire for more knowledge of economic behavior; in other words, it is a search for knowledge for its own sake. Moreover, even though much economic analysis *is* dominated by practical issues, this does not affect the methodology of the inquiry. Historical circumstances give rise to some questions, but even here the analysis should be scientific.

The scientific study of economic phenomena is necessary for us to obtain a more systematic knowledge of the world around us. This knowledge is useful both for its own sake and in order to undertake economic policy. As we have stressed throughout this book, however, scientific methods alone are not enough.

If scientists and artists both engage in similar activities, why is it useful to distinguish between them? First, in spite of their similarities, Science and Art do, as we have argued, differ in their intended end-product. Second, they differ in their methods; this is an important point that will be discussed later.

ECONOMICS AS A SCIENCE

The popular image of what science entails is experimentation under laboratory conditions. Many students react negatively to the notion of the social *sciences* being scientific, not because they think that scientific analysis is inappropriate, but because they think it is impossible to develop scientific understanding in circumstances in which experimentation is not possible. On the other hand, not *all* of the natural

---

[2]It can also be argued that current concerns have affected the development of the physical sciences. Science in the sixteenth and seventeenth centuries drew its questions from astronomy, because accurate navigation was so important. Science in the eighteenth and nineteenth centuries was concerned with the behavior of energy, because industrial machinery needed power. For a deeper discussion of this point, see J. Bronowski, *Science and Human Values,* Revised Edition. (New York: Harper & Row, 1965.)

sciences are able to use experiments in laboratories. Some aspects of zoology, for example, by their very nature cannot be subject to experimentation. The observation of animal behavior in the wild is somewhat like observations made of the wheat market in Chicago. Of course, we may change phenomena simply by observing them, but this can also be a problem for the scientist in the laboratory. Astronomers also cannot use experiments in a laboratory, but they do use scientific methods to observe natural phenomena, to produce predictions, and to test them.

The aim of economic analysis as a scientific undertaking is to arrive at verifiable statements about the likely behavior of the variables under discussion. For this, models are indispensable. Isolation of various factors is vital to the process of discovery. While economists cannot usually isolate by using laboratory experiments, they do isolate by the selection of a specific question, the construction of a model, and the use of various statistical techniques.

What is the result of persistent scientific inquiry? In the grand sense, scientific understanding is unlikely to be a steady progression from error to truth, simply because the concept of "truth" varies over time. Views on what constitute the fundamental particles in physics have changed rapidly over the last fifty years. Questions and categories in any science are bound to change owing to altered perceptions and new understandings.

On a smaller scale, however, science is involved in a progression not because we know more about the truth, but because we are capable of gathering more information and of building more appropriate models to deal with particular questions. For example, we can learn more about the types of butterflies in a certain geographical area or about the nature of the demand for a certain commodity in a given market situation. To do this, we must build models.

If you still think that model-building is an unreasonable activity for the categorization of the behavior of people, then there are two ways of countering your objection. The first is to repeat the argument that there is some order in human behavior. For example, examine the situation at a football game. In the sports stadium, there may be laborers, doctors, fathers, brothers, and so forth, but in this situation they are all "spectators," and their behavior is likely to be determined more by which team they support than by whose brother they are.

If you still remain unconvinced of the possibility of isolating aspects of behavior for scientific analysis, then we must look for an alternative to science. The only real alternative is revelation. Although it is undoubtedly important for obtaining a sense of the universe in both an immediate and an ultimate sense, there is little reason to think that revelation would help in economic analysis.[3] We surely cannot believe that economists are more prone to revelation than other members of the community are.

REVELATION AND AUTHORITY

Although revelation is not used explicitly by investigators of phenomena in the social sciences, appeals to authority are quite commonly employed. These two alternatives to science are closely connected by their mutual refusal to test their statements by an appeal to the facts of the real world. They are also interrelated during the course of an investigation. Revelation produces the postulates of a "model," and applied logic produces conclusions that are then tested by appeals to authority—that is, they are tested by checking whether they agree with the opinion of some authority, such as Karl Marx, Adam Smith, or some other learned person (who is usually safely dead). This method of inquiry is not new. It was the usual method during the Middle Ages when the pursuit of knowledge was conducted by appeals to the authority of the ancients (often Plato or Aristotle). Debate was largely restricted to which of the ancients should be considered as *the* authority.

How does the use of imagination in modern scientific method differ from the use of revelation and appeals to authority? After all, the scientific method does seem to be similar to them. Imagination produces postulates and assumptions, and logic is applied to these to produce predictions, which are then tested against the evidence of the real world. The difference lies in the reliance of the scientific method on testing, which makes it possible to see whether the evidence of the real world confirms the usefulness of the classifications and the models developed by imaginative researchers. Scientific models are modified by appealing to the real world; models produced on the basis of revelation are only modified by appealing to some authority.

To some extent, we have come full circle, since appeal to authority is one of the methods employed by the humanities.

---

[3]Immediate: The world is wicked. Ultimate: God is the only salvation.

It is one of the ways in which literary criticism is conducted. Certain works of literature are compared with an ideal type developed over time by various authorities. While this is a legitimate and useful method for the humanities, it cannot tell us much about the real world. To discover something about the real world, there is no substitute for science.

FINAL WORDS

There is really no neat way to sum up a book such as this. The building of models in the pursuit of knowledge is not easy. There are *some* rules to follow. The assumptions and the postulates should be explicit, the categories should be unambiguous, the reasoning should be logical, the predictions should be produced and tested against new observations, and in the light of this testing, the model may or may not be modified. Model-building involves much more than simply following these rules, however. It often entails the development of new assumptions, postulates, and categories. This process cannot be taught; thus, this book has deliberately left many loose ends. Only in the practice of science will you perhaps be able to tie some of these ends yourself.

QUESTIONS

1. What distinction did J. S. Mill make between Science and Art? Can you identify the scientific and the artistic aspects of economics on the basis of Mill's distinction? Would you accept the distinction as still being valid?

2. In what ways is language a model?

3. "Scientific method is essential if we are to progress from error to truth." How would you interpret such a statement?

4. In the text, revelation has been contrasted to scientific methodology. Imagination, we have said, is essential for science to progress. If, however, we think of the story of Newton and the apple, Galileo and the lamp, or Watt and the steam kettle, "revelation" and "imagination" seem to be very much the same. Is the initial *contrast* still valid when seen in the light of actual scientific progress?

5. The word "imagination" is derived from "image." Thus, to use imagination is to produce an image. We also produce images by model-building, however. How, then, can we distinguish the use of imagination from the formal building of models?

QUESTIONS FOR DISCUSSION

A. Consider the following simple analogies frequently used in elementary discussions of social policy, and try to establish what they can and cannot show within the context in which they are normally applied:

(a) the ship of state

(b) the winds of change

(c) the scales of justice

Are there any dangers in making use of such simple analogies to analyze social policy?

B. In Chapter 2, it was argued that there are no "natural categories" in scientific analysis. Perhaps what should have been said was that there "should not be" natural categories, for several natural categories keep getting in the way of theorists (such as the idea that "capital" and "labor" are mutually exclusive, or the notion that the "proletariat" can be immediately identified). Can you think of other categories that receive similar treatment by commentators? Why do you think people persist in treating such categories as being natural? Does ideology play any part in supporting these categories?

C. Chapter 3 dealt with questions and answers, but it did not ask, "*Who* asks the questions?" This may, however, be related to the types of questions asked, and *ideology* plays a part in this. What is the role of ideology? Has ideology received adequate treatment in this book? Do the methods of recruitment and training of social scientists have any influence on the types of questions they ask?

D. "Value-free" economics was not a term we used when dealing with positive economics in Chapter 4; yet some would equate the *idea* of positive economics with "value-free" economics. There has been talk of "dispassionate positivism" (sometimes considered a vice and sometimes a virtue). Is positive economics value-free? Do you think that the idea of value-free economics has any validity? Is it an ideal type?

E. "Model-building involves distortions. The real problem in constructing models lies not so much with individual assumptions (such as rationality and economic man), but in the ideological predispositions of the model-builder. Whereas the social scientists will look at neoclassical models and understand the 'as if' condition (especially when dealing with perfect competition), the layman will assume that the neoclassical world is full of perfectly competitive markets. Chapter 4 did not deal with the 'Classical/Neoclassical/Keynesian/Marxist' split in economic model constructs, *but* it might be argued that here at least the 'limitations in perception' do seem to fall into precise groups. Here we can look to the classifications to help us examine the usefulness of a particular model. At least this approach would help us to isolate the ideological predispositions of the original model-builder." Discuss.

F. "What we want from a model is both descriptive accuracy (in the sense that processes in the model reflect those in reality) *and* predictive accuracy. We accept 'positive' economics as only a second-best solution. The 'state of the arts' is the most pressing reason for accepting 'positive' economics." Discuss.

G. "One of the major dangers in mathematical economics is that the elegance of the math will tend to become more important than the relevance of the model." Is this a reasonable criticism of mathematical economics? Is there scope in economics for "pure" and "applied" subdivisions, as in other disciplines? What do you think the authors of this book would argue? Would you agree?

H. "If social science really involves as much judgment, imagination, or intuition as implied in Chapter 9, then "Science" is an ideal for the social investigator rather than an established fact. It should be called Social Studies and left at that." What do you think?

I. Play a game of Mastermind (Invicta Plastics [U.S.A.] Ltd.,), and try during or after the game to state any initial and subsequent assumptions, hypotheses, and propositions that you made or estimated to solve the problem posed by the game. Did you estimate statistical probabilities?

J. The feudal system was the main form of social organization in Europe during the Middle Ages. It was strictly hierarchical, and all land was nominally owned by the king. He granted land to the lords in exchange for military service; they in turn granted some land to lesser barons, again in exchange for military service. Similarly, peasants were granted land in exchange for military or agricultural services.

Some economists in the field of development have attempted to use the feudal system as a model to analyze the behavior of farmers in developing countries. Would you expect this to be a fruitful exercise? What light could it throw on these new problems? What problems might be encountered in the use of this model?

FURTHER READING

Abercrombie, M. L. J. *The Anatomy of Judgement.* London: Hutchinson, 1960.
 Traces out the ways in which selection and judgment are involved in the receipt of information from an outside stimulus. Chapter VI deals with observation, which turns out to be a very complex process.

Archibald, G. C. "Chamberlin vs. Chicago." *Review of Economic Studies,* No. 78, October, 1961, pp. 2–28.
 Positive economists are taken to task in this essay for not applying their own methodological recipe to the analysis of monopolistic competition. Once students have been introduced to the arguments, a rewarding essay, though difficult.

Archibald, G. C. "The State of Economic Science." *British Journal for the Philosophy of Science,* Vol. X, No. 37, May, 1959, pp. 58–69.
 A difficult essay, probably meant only for the enthusiast. Deals with the nature of assumptions and is a critical review of Koopman's essay.

Archibald, G. C., and Lipsey, R. *An Introduction to a Mathematical Treatment of Economics.* 2nd ed. London: Weidenfeld and Nicolson, 1972.
 A mathematical economics book that significantly advances the reader's ability to manipulate economic problems. Very good on setting up and extending basic economic models.

Bronowski, J. *Science and Human Values.* Revised edition. New York: Harper & Row, 1965.
 A readable and thought-provoking discussion of the practices of Science and Art, and of the interaction between the values of Science and those of society.

Chorley, R. J. and Haggett, P. (Eds.) *Models in Geography.* London: Methuen and Co. Ltd., 1967.
 Deals with a variety of theoretical models used in geography. The chapters dealing with everyday models such as the map raise interesting questions.

Coase, R. H. "Marshall on Method." *Journal of Law and Economics,* Vol. XVIII (1), April, 1975.

A straightforward review of Marshall's opinions on methodology. Of particular interest is the section on Marshall on mathematics.

Downs, A. *An Economic Theory of Democracy.* New York: Harper & Row, 1957.
Extends the application of economics into the field of political analysis. It is useful in that it shows the importance of the choice/scarcity problem, the cost of information, and so forth.

Emmet, D., and MacIntyre, A. *Sociological Theory and Philosophical Analysis.* London: Macmillan & Co., 1970.
A collection of essays largely speculating on the comparability of knowledge in the natural sciences. The language of the essays is difficult for beginning students, although Chapters 1 and 2 should be understandable. The bibliography is also useful for sociologists and social anthropologists.

Eraut, M. *Fundamentals of Arithmetic.*
Fundamentals of Elementary Algebra.
Fundamentals of Intermediate Algebra.
New York: McGraw-Hill, 1970.
If you feel weak in any aspects of mathematics, these books will help. A programmed learning approach is used.

Fisher, F. M., and Ando, A. "Two Theorems on *Ceteris Paribus* in the Analysis of Dynamic Systems." *American Political Science Review*, Vol. 56, No. 1, March, 1962.
Deals with what happens to the validity of predictions when "ceteris paribus" assumptions are made for variables that have some influence on the problem being studied. A difficult essay, best left until the student has achieved confidence in handling simple models.

Friedman, M. "The Methodology of Positive Economics." In *Essays in Positive Economics.* Chicago: University of Chicago Press, 1953.
For a long time the basic statement of the scope and the method of positive economics. Particular attention is paid to the role of assumptions in economic analysis and the extent to which assumptions are or are not realistic. For new students, the essay is difficult, mainly owing to terminological difficulties — the word model, for example, is not used.

Hansen, A. H. *Guide to Keynes.* New York: McGraw-Hill, 1953.
A useful formulation of the Keynesian system for new readers.

Johnson, H. G. "The Economic Approach to Social Questions." *Economica*, Vol. XXXV, No. 137, February, 1968, pp. 1–21.
A very useful essay for new students. Johnson shows how fairly basic economic tools can be used to throw light on social and economic problems. The analysis is mainly of British problems, but the demonstration can be easily followed by students with other backgrounds. The "feel" of the work is important.

Karmel, P. H., and Polasek, M. *Applied Statistics for Economists.* 3rd ed. London: Pitmans, 1970.
A useful introduction for students without a strong mathematical background.

Katouzian, M. A. "Scientific Method and Positive Economics." *Scottish Journal of Political Economy,* Vol. XXI, No. 3, November, 1974.
A highly critical discussion of the methodology of positive economics. The author points out that no major economic hypothesis has been tested, refuted, and subsequently abandoned.

Koestler, A. *The Sleepwalkers.* London: Hutchinson, 1959.
A readable account of the historical development of astronomy.

Koopmans, T. C. "The Construction of Economic Knowledge." In *Three Essays on the State of Economic Science.* New York: McGraw-Hill, 1957.
A discussion of the role of postulates in the development of economic theory. Difficult, but worth reading.

Kuhn, T. S. *The Structure of Scientific Revolutions.* 2nd ed. Chicago: University of Chicago Press, 1970.
A lucid and logical, though controversial, discussion of the idea that scientific activity is typified not by a steady progression from error to truth, but by periods of steady accumulation of facts interrupted by periods of crisis that result in changed ways of looking at the world.

Marshall, A. *Principles of Economics: An Introductory Volume.* 8th ed. London: Macmillan & Co., 1922.
Many students are surprised to discover that "it's all in Marshall." Check his use of the analogy of trees and business firms.

Mill, J. S. *Essays on Some Unsettled Questions of Political Economy.* London: Longmans, 1874.
Mill spotted many problems in the way in which economics and reality interact. This collection of essays is of more than historical interest and is well worth study by the highly motivated student.

Nagel, E. "Assumptions in Economic Theory." *American Economic Review Papers and Proceedings,* Vol. 53, 1963.
A useful guide to reading Friedman's essay. In this short paper, Nagel clarifies Friedman's argument about the role of assumptions and spells out the various ways in which an assumption may be unrealistic.

Popper, K. *Conjectures and Refutations.* 3rd ed. London: Routledge and Kegan Paul, 1969.
A highly learned but readable analysis of how scientific knowledge grows. Refutation rather than verification of conjectures is seen as the goal of science.

Robbins, L. *The Nature and Significance of Economic Science.* 2nd ed. London: Macmillan & Co., 1952.
The starting point of most discussions on the nature of economics. It examines the methodology of economics and defines the area of study in terms of the choice/scarcity problem. In dealing with "propositions," the work is somewhat dated, but in other areas (particularly in dealing with "time"), the work is surprisingly modern and well worth reading.

Robinson, J. *An Essay on Marxian Economics.* London: Macmillan & Co., 1966.

The introduction is useful, because it illustrates the extent to which Marx's view of the important questions to be asked of capitalism differs from the questions of conventional economists.

Robinson, J. *Economic Philosophy.* Harmondsworth: Penquin Books Ltd., 1964.

Reviews major areas of economic thought. Students should find the first chapter on "Metaphysics, Morals and Science" useful. The effective use of analogy on pp. 19–23 should be noted.

Schultz, T. W. *Transforming Traditional Agriculture.* New Haven: Yale University Press, 1964.

An economics book without mathematics. If you read it, see M. Lipton's critique of the book in "The Theory of the Optimising Peasant." (Journal of Development Studies.)

Stark, W. *The Philosophical Foundations of Classical Economics.* London: Kegan Paul, 1943.

An old-fashioned work, but it raises many interesting questions about the basis of economic discussions. The argument may seem dated to modern readers, but Stark's work does promote thought.

Watson, J. D. *The Double Helix.* Harmondsworth: Penguin Books Ltd., 1970.

A view of scientific research that shows the extent to which imagination, individual personality and what is usually understood as the scientific approach have a part to play.

Yamane, T. *Statistics: An Introduction Analysis.* 2nd ed. New York: Harper & Row, 1967.

Makes use of mathematical analysis but is very useful for more advanced study. New students should follow the author's advice and stick to the earlier chapters.

Yeomans, K. A. *Applied Statistics: Statistics for the Social Scientist,* Vols. 1 and 2. Harmondsworth: Penguin Books Ltd., 1968.

A useful book, especially designed for social science students. It leads gently from elementary to more advanced statistical work.

INDEX